D0433824

So That Went Well...

So That Went Well...

UNPUBLISHED LETTERS
TO

The Daily Telegraph

EDITED BY KATE MOORE

WHITE LION PUBLISHING

First published in 2019 by White Lion Publishing
an imprint of The Quarto Group
The Old Brewery, 6 Blundell Street
London N7 9BH
United Kingdom

www.QuartoKnows.com

ISBN 978 0 71124 212 8
Ebook ISBN 978 0 71124 213 5

10 9 8 7 6 5 4 3 2 1

2023 2022 2021 2020 2019

Typeset in Mrs Eaves by SX Composing DTP, Rayleigh, Essex

Printed by CPI Group (UK) Ltd, Croydon, CR0 4YY

CONTENTS

INTRODUCTION

These are peculiar times. Over the last 12 months, there have been days when events have progressed so quickly that even the most avid observers have struggled to keep up. Red lines have melted away and Cabinet ministers jumped ship with alarming regularity; The Independent Group of rebel MPs assembled, morphed into Change UK and received their first electoral drubbing almost before readers had time to submit their own TIG-ger jokes. On the other hand, the Brexit process and the removal of Theresa May from Downing Street seemed to unfold in ultra-slow motion, likened, variously, to a no-fault divorce, continental drift and ejecting a particularly stubborn guest from a party.

If some readers started getting fidgety, dreaming of a time when they might no longer hear of backstops, unicorns or cans being kicked down roads, others plunged in with their own ideas to break the stalemate, or at least to provide some light relief. Could Noel Edmonds' expertise on *Deal or No Deal* be brought to bear? What might the divided Commons learn from the 13th-century struggle to elect a new pope? And how might vegetarians cope with a salad shortage, should tomatoes and courgettes be held at the border after a hard exit?

There was also, thank goodness, plenty of life beyond Brexit. Come June, Mrs May was on her way out, leaving an overcrowded field of Tory hopefuls to battle for supremacy. The readers responded to tales of MPs' past misdemeanours with unexpected confessions of their own; speculated as to Boris Johnson's prospects in a *Strictly* dance-off for the premiership, and commiserated with Jeremy Hunt as his

surname was once again mispronounced by broadcasters.
Away from the Westminster circus, they found time to
weigh in on subjects ranging from climate change to Marie
Kondo and from D-Day to the fire at Notre-Dame, devised
elegant solutions to the problem of drones over Gatwick,
and celebrated the arrival of another royal baby while
pondering whether new parents the Duke and Duchess of
Sussex might be fans of *Educating Archie*. Add to this their
perennially entertaining takes on everything from sex to
The Archers, the perils of and occasional advantages to getting
old, bald, fat or merely cross, and the cautionary tale of
the minor celebrity who once tried his luck in a traditional
country pub - and you have an alternative view of the year
that should, I hope, make sense out of the chaos, and raise
a laugh when only laughter will do.

This is the 11th instalment in the series of hitherto
unpublished letters, and my first at the helm. I am
grateful to Matt, to the Letters Editor Christopher
Howse, to everyone at Quarto and to my predecessor
Iain Hollingshead for his wise parting advice. And I
am particularly grateful, of course, to the letter-writers
themselves, without whose sublime sense of the ridiculous
the world would be much the poorer.

Kate Moore
London SW1

FAMILY
TRIALS AND
TRIBULATIONS

Adventures in Nappy Valley

SIR - Ant Middleton (of Everest climbing fame) complains that he gets twitchy if he isn't involved in some exciting and adventurous exploit. May I suggest his next one? Mrs Middleton goes away for ten days to do a course on Latin epigraphy/Greek cuisine/underwater t'ai-chi, leaving him to feed, clothe and occupy their four children. He will be allowed only one trip to McDonald's and one to A&E and will be filmed 24 hours a day.

Afterwards, he may feel the need to live on South Georgia for a while.

Susan M. Walton
Gateshead, Surrey

SIR - My son-in-law has just purchased a sterilising kit for our newborn granddaughter. One of the items in the box was described as a "teat tong".

I always thought he was a disc jockey.

Michael Cattell
Chester

SIR - Russell Brand is only one of many men with an aversion to changing nappies. A Swiss friend of mine summed up his experience as follows: "I have only changed a nappy on three occasions and hit the jackpot every time."

Roger Whiteway
Kibworth, Leicestershire

SIR - When my husband was left holding a baby with a dirty nappy, he drove several miles to his ex-wife and persuaded her to change the child. Luckily she was also the baby's godmother; presidential thinking.

Caroline Charles-Jones
Newport, Monmouthshire

SIR - A study has found that having children will disrupt your sleep "for at least six years".

Dream on. It's more like 26 years, as any parent will testify after lying awake listening for adult offspring to return from a nightclub at three in the morning.

Richard Cheeseman
Yateley, Hampshire

Can't be too careful

SIR - Some years ago plastic packaging from a recently purchased item suggested: "to avoid suffocation keep away from children." So for a long time I did so, only having my two sons when I was well into my forties.

Good advice.

Robert Moore
Bloxham, Oxfordshire

SIR - I am concerned that the Meccano set I recently bought for my grandson does not have a health warning on the box.

Surely it should say "may contain nuts".

Peter Mulford
Brentford, Middlesex

SIR - Apparently the slogan "Approved by mums" on packets of Coco Pops discriminates against fathers. It is to be changed to "Approved by parents".

Does this not discriminate against orphans?

Peter Harper
Salisbury, Wiltshire

Years of service

SIR - When my young man spoke to my dad about marriage, way back in 1960, my dad said: "Boy, you deserve a medal". The same young man received a long service medal in 2010. Assuming we are still together in 2020, what do I get for him then?

Ann Barnes
Beckenham, Kent

SIR - My wife and I were cast as the back end and front end of the horse respectively in the local pantomime.

I believe our surname helped us to secure the part.

John and Mary Dobbin
Buckingham

SIR - When my wife and I ran a little B&B some years back we kept a visitors' book. A lifelong friend came to stay, leaving in our visitors' book: "Nice lady. Pity about the bloke."

We left it in - explaining, if it was seen, the reason behind it.

Michael Hooper
Thorley, Hertfordshire

Accounting for tastes

SIR – When I, a competent cook, left home at 18, I took
a fruit cake, tea, coffee, biscuits and skimmed milk.
My sons left with an addition of rice, pasta, tomato puree,
seasonings and many tins of baked beans.

Waitrose suggests a starter kit of vegetable bouillon
powder, cider vinegar, organic Italian seasoning, rose
harissa and an organic soy sauce.

The times they are a-changing.

Sheelagh James
Lichfield, Staffordshire

SIR – I am both an avid reader of the cooking section and
an exponent of its recipes. However, I do tend to venture
off-piste and indulge in experimental cooking of a style
inspired by Keith Floyd.

Having endured a weekend of their father's cooking,
including sausage rolls that could combat coastal erosion
and triple-cooked chips that were more hazmat than
Heston, my long-suffering sons were positively begging for
something ready-prepared from the supermarket.

Chris Bands
Farnham, Surrey

SIR – My late beloved mama, upon marriage becoming
the owner of an Aga, measured all cooking according to
the yardstick of: "When it's brown it's done, and when it's
black, it's b-----ed."

Felicity Foulis Brown
Bramley, Hampshire

SIR - My lovely wife, a fabulous cook, died recently, leaving me with over 40 cookery books. I have skimmed through them and chosen one recipe from each to make in her memory whenever I feel ambitious enough. So far I haven't poisoned anyone - but I still have around 30 more chances.

Don Webber
Bembridge, Isle of Wight

SIR - I have 36 cookery books. My husband says my oven has healed up.

He is not wrong.

Diana Whiteside
Berkhamsted, Hertfordshire

The excuse that won't wash

SIR - Earlier this week, my wife and I went for our flu jabs. The nurse (female) saw us both together. Having explained about possible side-effects, she stated that after receiving the jab ladies should refrain from doing the washing-up for at least 24 hours.

I have no medical qualifications; can any reader confirm that this is a genuine side-effect?

George Brown
Manchester

SIR - We have been watering the garden with bathwater and "grey" tap water.

When making my daily cuppa, I noticed a lack of teaspoons. Upon investigation, I found the missing items

underneath the rose bushes in the front garden, where
my husband had been diligently throwing the washing-up
water.

Debbie Martin
Princes Risborough, Buckinghamshire

SIR - My husband and I each do our own laundry ever since
the day my husband said: "Darling, you haven't hung my
socks up properly on the airer."

I thoroughly recommend it.

Mary Gorman
Warrington, Cheshire

Under covers operation

SIR - A scientific study has found that on average British
married men had a stronger grip than men who were
widowed or never married. Could the difference be that
married men have to grip the quilt every night, or lose it?

Bruce Stratton
Ongar, Essex

SIR - You report that a woman is suing a bed company for
injury sustained when a bed on which she was having sex
collapsed.

When on my honeymoon at a hotel in Corfu in 1972
the iron-framed bed on which I was lying collapsed with a
resounding crash. The broken furniture was removed and
left in the corridor for the rest of our stay - much to the
embarrassment of my wife and I and the amusement of the
chambermaids. I never contemplated litigation as I was too

ashamed to admit I was only reading *The Daily Telegraph* at the time of the incident.

Dr Martin Henry
Chelmsford, Essex

Natural selection

SIR – Research suggests that many women are highly attracted to Alpha males, and particularly so when at their most fertile. However, they also recognise that Alpha males can be egotistical, aggressive or unreliable partners in the long term. Hence the optimum strategy is to secure Alpha gene material via a brief liaison, and then find a Beta male to marry and to raise the offspring.

I'm not sure this reflects very well on anyone involved, but Nature is driving and we are really just along for the ride.

Toby Varney
Wiveliscombe, Somerset

SIR – Sarah Knapton reports on a new study into how men "strive to learn how things work through their underlying parts".

Perhaps they would be better advised to use their brains.

Paul Machin
Cheltenham, Gloucestershire

Women put their feet down

SIR – When I left university in the early Eighties and began working, my grandmother gave me some invaluable advice on how to deal with unwanted attention. Wear heels and use them. When the individual with wandering hand trouble has difficulty believing his attentions are unwelcome, a well-placed stiletto heel is a very effective way of communicating the fact.

Alison Crane
London SW15

SIR - The actress Kristen Bell has issues with the prince kissing a sleeping Snow White.

I'm more concerned that Snow White would want to live on her own with seven single men.

Lintie Gibson
Melrose, Roxburghshire

SIR - I am glad that wolf-whistling is not (yet) considered a hate crime. To me it caused much amusement as I walked along a wall in Ireland beside a building site. There were several lots of wolf-whistling, but when I came to a gap in the wall the whistling stopped. I was six months pregnant and the bump had made its appearance.

Polite builders and no harm.

Sue Samuelson
Chipping Campden, Gloucestershire

SIR - Surely wolf-whistling should be listed as a "love crime". If the whistlee is distressed by the event, the whistler should be punished by taking her out to a supervised dinner - and he should pick up the tab.

Michael Bennett
Godalming, Surrey

SIR - What it comes down to is this. Any man who grabs a

woman by the bum is an inadequate prat. Always has been. Always is. Always will be.

Peter Wyton
Gloucester

Changing of the seasons

SIR - Though the calendar says it is January, Mother Nature knows better. Is it not time to introduce a leap month to get us back into synchronisation with her?

Andy Rocks
Camberley, Surrey

SIR - When is the start of spring? Is it the Met Office's 1 March or is it the spring equinox ? In my house it's the day when my wife allows me to remove the electric blanket from the bed. This year it is today, 27 March. Happy spring.

John Rowlands
Harpenden, Hertfordshire

SIR - I heard my first cuckoo on Puttenham Common in Surrey this morning (15 April). He must have heard the weather forecast for the Easter weekend.

Sue Gowar
Elstead, Surrey

SIR - Are there any more worrying words than a man wandering into the garden saying "I think I might do a bit of strimming"?

Zanzie Griffin
Cullompton, Devon

SIR - A helpful student in Buxton once instantly and spontaneously solved the problem of our iced-up windscreen. It was a successful no-hands action, which involved jumping on the bonnet of the car and adopting a hip-wiggle reminiscent of Elvis Presley in the film *Jailhouse Rock*. Fortunately for the inspired student, no police were out on the beat that night.

Geoff Milburn
Barnard Castle, County Durham

In love and war

SIR - With the start of a new month, one is reminded of the traditional "pinch, punch, first of the month", to which the response would be "a punch and a kick for being so quick". This was then followed by "a slap in the eye for being so sly". Does anyone know if there are further couplets, as the whole affair descends into open warfare?

David Jones
Canterbury, Kent

SIR - On 1 November, as the *Today* programme announced the date, my husband and I both attacked each other.

I am not badly injured and am happy to report that this tradition still exists in Surrey.

Shirley Burrill
Churt, Surrey

SIR - I always feel sorry for the hopeful Valentine bouquets on display in the supermarkets. If they're lucky, they will be bought.

Otherwise their fate, by the end of the week, is to be reduced, and stuffed into a corner in a draught.

Bunny Plat
Caernarfon, Gwynedd

SIR - Given the unstoppable rise of antibiotic-resistant gonorrhoea, it is unfortunate that Shane Watson chose to abbreviate Valentine's Day to VD.

Professor Gareth Williams
Berkeley, Gloucestershire

Tricksy treats

SIR - With the volume of treats (mainly sweets) being handed out on Halloween it can't be long before the practice is condemned for fuelling the obesity crisis.

Phillip Wade
Cheltenham, Gloucestershire

Earlier every year

SIR – When I went to the newsagent this morning for my paper, I knew Christmas must be close, because on the counter was an open box of Cadbury's creme eggs.

Jeremy Bateman
Luton, Bedfordshire

SIR – Is there any more depressing sight than a Christmas gift set in October? Come to that, is there anyone who would be thrilled with a miniature bottle of whisky and two golf balls?

Patsie Goulding
Reigate, Surrey

SIR – Seen in a local store window: "BLACK FRIDAY – ENDS TUESDAY".

Janet Kay
York

SIR – At my local supermarket, a man in his forties was being pushed in his wheelchair with his carer, and he was singing what sounded like carols at the top of his voice. He lit up the whole aisle with sunshine. So there is something to say for a commercial Christmas.

I wonder what happened when he got to the Halloween stuff.

Simon Roff
Helston, Cornwall

No really, you shouldn't have

SIR - Christmas gift catalogues are arriving in my porch with regularity.

If you are reading this, Father Christmas, I will not be too disappointed if you forget to bring:

A singing Frisbee

Deer deterrent

Ukulele for beginners

A build-your-own football stadium

A plastic dinosaur skull or

A fart extinguisher.

Dave Alsop
Churchdown, Gloucestershire

SIR - A few years ago I received a Christmas gift from my wife of a small "artisan" sack of porridge accompanied by a hand-turned, polished piece of beech, which, according to the attached label, was a spurtle (a traditional Scottish implement for stirring porridge). I know the Scots are a canny lot, and so I salute their enterprise in being able to part sensible people from their cash for what I can only describe as a stick.

Mike Norman
Penperlleni, Monmouthshire

Glad tidings

SIR - I can report that this year's Christmas cards are predominantly side-hinged, enabling them to occupy horizontal surfaces without resort to the clothesline approach.

It avoids the gradual legs-spread effect and is most welcome.

Mark Rand
Settle, North Yorkshire

SIR - I have been lamenting the lack of robins on our Christmas cards this year. The llama we have just received is no substitute.

Ros Mackay
Helston, Cornwall

SIR - When my husband remarked of a Christmas card adorned with six robins that "they are very nice turkeys", I knew it was time to book him a New Year appointment with a well-known high-street opticians.

Jane Moth
Snettisham, Norfolk

Extra stuffing

SIR - Health experts have released a list of the exercise needed to work off various festive treats. It would surely be a service to the public if they were to list the length of time one must spend lying on the sofa in order to burn off the equivalent calories.

Peter Harper
Lover, Wiltshire

SIR - After several years of diminishing returns we have, this year, managed to get all our silver sixpences back from the Christmas pudding.

I had been considering an X-ray machine to check our guests' digestive systems.

Ian Stewart
Crowborough, East Sussex

SIR - I knew I was into the swing of things on Christmas Day when I asked my husband and mother-in-law for their technique in putting their crowns on over their antlers.

Vanessa Travers
Epsom, Surrey

Green pledges up in smoke

SIR - How dangerous is the particulate matter that would arise from my solely burning the paper upon which government policy initiatives are written, rather than using coal or seasoned wood?

Dr Bertie Dockerill
Bishop Auckland, County Durham

SIR - Given Michael Gove's latest pledge, should we now expect a wood burner scrappage scheme?

Sue McFadzean
Swansea

SIR - The advisers who urge us to keep thermostats at 19C appear to have failed to recognise another serious risk to climate overheating.

This will be caused by the steam coming from the ears of men, like my own dear husband, who think that heating does not need to be over 15C.

Yours, clad in layers of wool.

Gillian Badcock
Hythe, Kent

Life in plastic

SIR – With the news that there is enough plastic to give the earth another layer and that we seem to be entering an era of climate change, may I be the first to suggest that we christen this new epoch the Plasticine Age.

Jon Price
Upton, Wirral

SIR   Today I purchased a bunch of small bananas. Printed on the plastic bag which contained them were the words "organic/working with nature".

Linda Major
London SW15

SIR – We are about to embark upon using seaweed instead of plastic as a food wrapper.
I take it the supply of seaweed is infinite.

Audrey Pitchforth
Hemel Hempstead, Hertfordshire

SIR – My husband has a container that is labelled "Junk Too Good to Throw Away".

Susan Fleck
Cheltenham, Gloucestershire

The wrong sort of message

SIR - Royal Mail has asked people to stop sending them used crisp packets as these delay sorting. In fact we sorters often have to deal with much worse things. One night I had to fish out the following: the remains of a fish and chip supper, a pair of lady's jeans, then a pair of knickers and a used condom. Someone had obviously had a good time!

> **Ted Shorter**
> Tonbridge, Kent

SIR - Am I alone in being frustrated by postal workers' frequent inability to shut a gate they opened a minute earlier? Surely "How to shut a gate" cannot be more than a two-day course.

> **Peter H. York**
> Daventry, Northamptonshire

Privy Counsel

SIR - The demise of our magnificent Victorian-era toilets - some of which were of Gothic proportions - is a great shame. The sheer joy of being able to aim at the insect embossed in the slab urinal, while admiring the ceramic interior, is now gone forever.

> **Robert Guttridge**
> Sheffield

SIR - Why does my loo paper fall to the floor from the holder without a cuddly puppy pulling it off?

The paper is smaller in width and length. No less expensive.

Mary Tobias
Eastbourne, East Sussex

SIR – *There's always queues for ladies' loos,*
  It really is a bore.
  'Twould serve them right if out of spite
  We did it on the floor.

Jacqui Harbour
High Wycombe, Buckinghamshire

I'm with stupid

SIR – I was relieved to read the feature article titled: "Why smart people do stupid things". For most of my life I have done stupid things and made stupid decisions and my three older brothers have delighted in putting this down to my stupidity. To discover that, in fact, this is due instead to being very smart is wonderfully reassuring. I look forward to letting them know.

Jo Marchington
Ashtead, Surrey

SIR – Useful everyday law lexicon:
  This is receiving our immediate attention – We've lost the file.
  We are referring to counsel – We don't know what to do next.
  We will use our best endeavours – We're not going to agree to what you want.

Rev David J. Addington
March, Cambridgeshire

SIR - A work colleague always used to answer his office phone by saying: "I don't know anything about it, I wasn't there at the time, I didn't do it and even if I did do it you told me to. How can I help you?"

Richard Anning
Chipping Norton, Oxfordshire

SIR - In the old days the village looked after the village idiot; nowadays these people work for the council.

David Brearley
Rawdon, West Yorkshire

Good game, good game

SIR - The residents of Costessey in Norfolk - who are being terrorised by an aggressive pheasant - may be pleased to learn that there is a simple solution to their problems. It's called a casserole.

Charles Smith-Jones
Landrake, Cornwall

SIR - Having observed my wife on a road trip - and given the obvious increase in magpies on roads since general licences to control bird pest species were revoked - I am very concerned that insufficient attention is being paid to the biggest threat this decision is causing.

As she chants "Good morning Mrs Magpie" and then spits three times over her left shoulder each time she encounters one of these birds, it is clear that road safety is being severely compromised.

Michael Vaughan-Fowler
Reading, Berkshire

SIR - I have just run over and killed a pigeon. Luckily I
hold a licence — a driving licence. Does this count?

George Bastin
Stroud, Gloucestershire

Hounded out of town

SIR - The naturalist Chris Packham has invited hunters to
pursue him rather than foxes.

Would they please oblige him by chasing this over-
opinionated expert-on-everything down a hole, but refrain
from digging him out.

Carmichael A. Thomas
Wellingborough, Northamptonshire

SIR - In the spirit of inclusivity local hunts should
encourage vegans to take part in their sport. It could be
adapted to their sensibilities and a nut roast or a tofu
burger could provide the scent for the following pack.
The intolerant in pursuit of the unappetising.

James Longman
Christchurch, Dorset

SIR - I retain my membership of the National Trust
through gritted teeth.

I am on the hunt for a suitable Get Well card.

Sally Eyre
Wotton-under-Edge, Gloucestershire

Legging it

SIR - We have reached a windy but golden autumn; but lives are at risk. Spiders are already in trouble, stranded in a landscape of foothills becoming vertical climbs from which there is no escape. We call it the bath.

To free this amenity of the spider, dangle a piece of toilet paper in its path. It will soon climb aboard. Release the spider from a nearby open window and watch it parachute gently and safely towards the ground. There will be a feel-good factor in this for both you and the spider.

Barry Bond
Leigh-on-Sea, Essex

SIR - When my wife or daughter shout that there is a giant spider in the bathroom or kitchen I go to get rid of it, but by the time I arrive I have to use a magnifying glass to find it.

Do other readers suffer from this breed of shrinking spiders?

Keith Baker
Worthing, West Sussex

A brush with danger

SIR -The RSPCA has warned against using human toothpaste to clean your dog's teeth.

Visiting us for the weekend a few years ago, our daughter mistakenly used our dog's toothpaste on our then four-

year-old grandson. He came to no harm, but did venture
the comment: "I thought it tasted a bit funny."

Don Haines
Telford, Shropshire

SIR - I wouldn't dream of attempting to clean my
Jack Russell's teeth. Her veterinary notes simply state
"WATCH". Holding her at the vet's can be like holding a
bucket of water without the bucket.

Rosie Harden-Vane
Holywell, Northumberland

SIR - Judith Woods is lucky to have accommodating dogs
come bedtime. My own miniature dachshund insists on
lying horizontally under my duvet, leaving me clinging to
the edge. I meekly get out of bed, walk around and get in on
the other side rather than risk disturbing her. Nevertheless
she is my perfect bedfellow and I hers.

Jessica Church
Evenley, Northamptonshire

My Father's house has many rooms

SIR - My wife and I recently attended a funeral and queued
to write a message of condolence in the book that had been
set up in the entrance to the church.

At the end of the ceremony the church warden approached
us all to thank us for signing up for cleaning duties.

Mick Pilsworth
London W8

SIR - Rather than emphasise God's asexuality, I wish that Archbishop Justin Welby had stressed instead that men, males and fathers are not God.

Rob Reynolds
Staplefield, West Sussex

SIR - You quote Archbishop Justin Welby as stating that "employers in every sector need unions to keep them doing justice". What on earth does that mean?

Gobbledygook is best reserved for the pulpit.

Kenneth Preston
Hillsborough, County Down

SIR - I do not believe in the Labour Party. Will I be welcome in the Church of England?

Brian Farmer
Chelmsford, Essex

Better to give than to receive

SIR - My mother and some of the local ladies collect for a major national charity and last weekend did so at a local shopping centre. The money raised was the laudable sum of £660.

I have just worked out that this will pay the salary of the CEO of that charity for one and a half days.

Geoff Smith
Gretna, Dumfriesshire

SIR - A study by the Office for National Statistics (ONS) has concluded that money does not make people happy. If this is true, perhaps we should cut the salaries of the ONS staff.

J.A. Dupont
Clevedon, Somerset

SIR - Money can't buy happiness, but it enables one to be miserable in comfort.

S. Rosebery
Croydon, Surrey

Small screen, big headache

SIR - Modern TVs are far too complex. Oh for the Fifties: three knobs for on/off, loudness and brightness, plus mysterious things called horiz. and vert. hold, which Father forbade us to touch.

Mike Brooks
Sutton Coldfield

SIR - Yesterday, having made one of my infrequent visits to London, I was returning home by train.

As soon as she sat down the young lady sitting opposite started tapping on her phone. She was immediately outbid by her neighbour, who produced two phones.

However, they were both completely trumped by a fellow traveller using two phones and a tablet (with earphones).

I felt very out of touch.

Andy Ritchie
Loxwood, West Sussex

SIR - This morning, upon entering a public convenience in York, I saw a man with one hand under the hand dryer, while texting with the other. Is there any conceivable situation in which a mobile phone can't be used?

Andrew Sturmey
Selby, North Yorkshire

A tangled web

SIR - I can appreciate the difficulty in spotting fake videos online. However, there are certain circumstances when spotting them should be easy. Be sceptical of any video in which Donald Trump is speaking sensibly, Sir Philip Green appears charming, or any instance where a politician appears to be speaking openly and honestly.

Gray A. Pratt
Banchory, Aberdeenshire

SIR - The consumer group Which? has concluded after a lengthy investigation that Amazon is awash with fake five-star reviews, despite the company claiming it has measures in place to detect, identify and remove both fraudulent reviews and the bot accounts used to generate them.

In other news, grass is green, water is wet, and cats like cardboard boxes.

Mark Boyle
Johnstone, Renfrewshire

SIR - Without Tim Berners-Lee's invention of the World Wide Web, I would not have known about the millions of dollars that I have won, been awarded or been asked to look after over the years.

Frank Bown
Epsom, Surrey

SIR - In his article on Japanese manga, Sam Leith suggested that it might not be a good idea to Google "tentacle porn". I wonder how many of your readers did the same as me and looked it up immediately. You do indeed learn something every day, and I shall now view manga with new eyes.

Jacqueline McCrindle
Prestwick, Ayrshire

Machine learning

SIR - I recently acquired my first mobile phone. It may not be "smart", but it is clever enough to out-smart me.

Phillip Crossland
Driffield, East Yorkshire

SIR - I find the idea of Alexa taking care of our elderly population rather frightening, as my Alexa does some very strange things - such as switching herself on when I am watching TV. This is quite unnerving and I certainly wouldn't want her looking after me.

Gill Sparkes
Richmond, Surrey

SIR - My dog's name is Dexter, and every time I call him my voice-activated assistant springs to attention. I'm thinking of buying her a collar and lead.

Paul Blundell
Daventry, Northamptonshire

SIR - I jokingly asked Siri if she could smell something.
   She proceeded to spell s-o-m-e-t-h-i-n-g. I was unsure if it was her hearing or my dodgy accent.

Henry Maj
Armitage, Staffordshire

SIR - I was recently compiling the minutes for my local Women's Institute on my iPad. One member had been complimented for her knitted socks and another for her knit and natter group. In both cases my Spellcheck suggested the word *knickers*. Has it got a one-track mind?

Dee Sykes
Haywards Heath, West Sussex

SIR - It is thought that in the future robots will take over many household chores, have rights and have to be paid.
   Looking ahead, will it be necessary to set up pension plans? They may also require medical insurance - although it would probably be better if they made friends with the washing machine and joined the same maintenance contract.

Anthony Gee
Leicester

SIR – Just because something is digital (e.g. Making Tax Digital) doesn't mean that it is modern and exciting. A digital rectal examination is neither.

Andrew Benham
London N14

Please replace the handset and try again

SIR – Having spent the last week trying, and failing, to resolve an issue with a large organisation, I have a suggestion for a new reality show. The format is that CEOs of large companies sit in a booth with access to the internet, their website and a phone and are given timed tasks relevant to their business.

Tasks can include finding a contact number for a specific department (and getting through), choosing an option number when none is relevant to your issue, tracking a lost package, changing a supplier and staying calm when the call cuts off for no reason after you've been waiting 42 minutes. The working title for my show is currently "How calm, reasonable people can be driven mad", but I appreciate that may have to change.

Jo Marchington
Ashtead, Surrey

SIR – My latest phone bill from BT is addressed to "Needs Updating G J Clifton".

Have they been speaking to my daughters?

Graham Clifton
Kingston upon Thames, Surrey

SIR - Congratulations to Alan Drever-Smith for transcribing the musical drivel inflicted upon him while waiting to speak to HMRC on the phone. I have to say the music played while waiting for a human reply at GB Energy was actually very pleasant. By the time I spoke to someone, I was in such a good mood I even forgave the company for mistakenly putting me on a list of debtors.

Fiona Wild
Cheltenham, Gloucestershire

SIR - I remember telephoning a company chief executive in the Nineties, and being put on hold. The holding music was by Dire Straits. I wish I had taken the hint and sold the shares, as the company went bust soon afterwards.

Shaun Whyte
Alnmouth, Northumberland

Location, location

SIR - If we are all to be microchipped, will that mean we will be able to find our wives in shopping centres?

Brian Christley
Abergele, Conwy

Educashun isn't wurking

SIR - I've just heard a teenager on Radio 4 say that the new GCSEs are "more harder". In that case, perhaps we should make them even more harder.

Patricia Harrison
Stebbing, Essex

SIR – I ask my football-mad eight-year-old grandson what he knew about 1066. He replied straight away that it was 900 years before England won the World Cup. Although he has recently done a project on the Titanic, he has yet to cover the Norman Conquest in his history lessons.

Peter Rayment
Preston Candover, Hampshire

SIR – I was interested by the recommendation that children should learn to count in base 12. A noble ambition and not without merit, but I was taught to count on my fingers and until we all have the extra appendages I doubt there will be a change.

Nick Pope
Reading, Berkshire

SIR – I was horrified to read Jane Shilling's article on modal verbs and frontal adverbials to realise, as a retired English teacher, that I have no idea what they are.

Jacqueline McCrindle
Prestwick, Ayrshire

Must try harder

SIR – Apparently Roger Daltrey, of The Who, thanks his former teacher Mr Kibblewhite for telling him he would never amount to anything in life. There must be many others who, determined to prove their teachers wrong, went on to be very successful.

Maybe more teachers should try this approach to encourage the next generation of school leavers.

Barbara Taylor
Alfrick, Worcestershire

SIR - Long school reports have been condemned as "incredibly burdensome" for teachers. This was not a problem in my day. A friend's report succinctly stated: "Tries but useless".

Mark Solon
London E1

SIR - When our four-year-old granddaughter was asked what her first day at school had been like, she replied: "It was OK but they forgot to teach me to read."

Robert Fowler
Stourport-on-Severn, Worcestershire

Degrees of separation

SIR - Hannah Betts admiringly recalls her fellow tutor at Oxford University telling a student to "Shut the f--- up". As - horror - a former polytechnic lecturer, I humbly acknowledge the unbridgeable pedagogic gap.

(Prof) Chris Barton
Stoke-on-Trent, Staffordshire

SIR - Back in the day, a first class degree would rightly only be achievable by the very brightest. I readily accepted the inevitability of a 2:2 in order to maintain my status as table football doubles champion.

Eleanor Patrick
Elsdon, Northumberland

SIR - One of the greatest inventions ever has to be the spreadsheet. How I wish it had existed when I read engineering at university. It would've given me many more valuable hours to conduct research - into beer.

Rob Sawyer
Southampton

Don't be so wet

SIR - Amid discussions on possible items to replace octopus terrine in an Oxford college dining hall, I suggest "Snowflake Soup". However, one possible problem would be how to heat it up.

Maurice des Forges
Saint Clement, Jersey

SIR - Search for "Radio 4 Brett Westwood - Natural Histories - Octopus". You will never want to eat octopus again. The programme's precis says they have "three hearts, copper blood, autonomous arms... and a formidable intelligence to match". Perhaps they should take over our Brexit negotiations.

Annabel Clements
Monmouth

SIR - The University of Manchester's Students' Union has reportedly passed a resolution outlawing clapping to avoid triggering anxiety. If aliens from outer space are monitoring our planet, they will be forced to conclude that there is no intelligent life on earth.

David Miller
Chigwell, Essex

Feeling poorly - or poor?

SIR - Your feature on colds and flu omitted the best test to differentiate between the two - the £20 note test.

If you are ill and see £20 in your garden and go and get it, it's a cold. If you can't be bothered, it's flu.

Steve Cattell
Grantham, Lincolnshire

SIR - I received a letter from the cardiology department at my local hospital on 8 March. The letter was dated 4 March and was for an appointment on the afternoon of 2 March.

Does the NHS have a time-travel department?

Stuart Oldham
Braunston in Rutland

SIR - I have always been confused by the logic behind homeopathy. Apparently the more diluted the liquid becomes, the more powerful and efficacious it gets and the greater the healing power.

Following that line of thought, if you take none at all, do you get better immediately?

Sue Ajax-Lewis
Walberton, West Sussex

SIR - The list of possible side-effects from the quinine sulphate tablets I take for night cramps include "death" - with the instruction that, should this occur, "treatment should be stopped and a doctor contacted straight away".

Unfortunately, there are no guidelines as to how I might do this.

Jill Fowler
Misterton, Somerset

One step at a time

SIR - Research shows that I can protect my bone strength by walking downhill rather than uphill, which makes bones fragile.

Could the researchers please tell me how I get back after descending the hill?

Barbara Goodman
Manchester

SIR - After my father died, I cleared the household loft and found a perfectly serviceable Zimmer frame which I had never seen either of my parents use. I took this down to the local hospital which accepted it with grace and gratitude. However, I never resolved the great question: if you need a Zimmer frame, why put it in the loft which you can't get to because you need a Zimmer frame?

Hilary Bentley
Alderney, Guernsey

This is a stitch-up

SIR - My husband underwent surgery to his shoulder following a skiing accident. He was advised by the consultant orthopaedic surgeon that this would be merely a "keyhole procedure". Given the 10 cm scar on my husband's shoulder, I can only assume that the consultant has a portcullis for a front door.

Diane Learmont-Hughes
Caldy, Wirral

SIR - I was fascinated to read your report that patients are being fitted with devices that failed testing in baboons.

When I had my pacemaker fitted on the NHS I wasn't even offered a banana in the recovery ward.

Ian McDougle
Farnham Common, Buckinghamshire

SIR - Noting concerns at the loss of medical students' ability to perform simple manual tasks, it is reported that "Imperial College has called in magicians to get students to learn how to listen intently and shape their hands to trick an audience".

Conversely, when I auditioned to become a member of The Magic Circle I employed my ability to tie a surgeon's knot one-handed and even used an ophthalmoscope to read the retina of my "subject" - discerning the very word he had just selected and read secretly from a book. Or so I had my audience believe.

A surgeon is a magician playing the part of a surgeon. Trust me, I am both.

Mr Richard Rawlins FRCS MMC
Dartmouth, Devon

Internal affairs

SIR - I have just heard someone say he is "scared someone will take his organs". He did not say if being given an organ also scares him.

Alan Sabatini
Bournemouth

SIR - The idea that space-age loos could send a report to one's smartphone based on analysis of one's "movements" assumes that every individual has their own personal loo.

If not, I can see panic setting in with familial ailments wrongly attributed.

Lynne Waldron
Woolavington, Somerset

SIR - It's a wonderful thing to have one's identity protected, but sometimes a little unnecessary. As I waited in a London hospital to go through the joys of a colonoscopy, a middle-aged gentleman was trying to check in. The attentive and kind receptionist asked him for ID. "I don't have any," he replied, "but I think it's rather unlikely anyone would want to pretend to be me and have a colonoscopy in my place."

Richard Grievson
Hungerford, Berkshire

Too many cooks

SIR - I believe that I have a solution to Britain's obesity problem.

Simply stop the transmission of all television programmes that have *Bake*, *Berry*, *Bikers*, *Chef*, *Naked*, *Nadiya*, *Nigella*, *Ramsay* or *Taste* in the title.

That should free up space for more reruns of *Dad's Army*.

David Ellis
Ellon, Aberdeenshire

SIR - My solution to obesity would be to have certain sections of the supermarket accessible only through a sliding door padlocked to restrict admission to persons under a specified girth.

And no sending the children in.

Reg W. Selfe
Benfleet, Essex

SIR - The news that ice-cream vans are no longer going to have tinny melodies is going to be a blow to those parents who have always told their children that the music is a sign that the ice-cream man has sold out.

Alan Stockwell
Smarden, Kent

When the chips are down

SIR - If keeping healthy means I have to make shepherd's pie with carrot mash instead of creamy potato, I think I will just risk the alternative.

Mrs B. Alexander
Turvey, Bedfordshire

SIR - If the government places a levy on red meat, does refusing a sausage become tax avoidance?

John Oxley
London E15

SIR - The over-consumption of plain water causes death through hyponatremia. Will our nanny state decide to increase tax on drinking water in order to prevent the occasional death?

Nigel Algar
Nottingham

SIR - Just when you think there cannot be any more ways in the universe to cook beetroot, Beetroot Wellington turns up.

Sandra Hawke
Andover, Hampshire

SIR - I find the furore over the presence of gelatin in Percy Pig sweets somewhat baffling.

Surely a vegan or vegetarian should be more concerned about their children eating something shaped like an animal about which it is often said the only inedible part is the squeak.

Diana Elsdon
New Malden, Surrey

SIR - When all else fails in food supply, we normally evolved meat-eating humans will be able to eat vegans, but not the reverse.

Davina Elaine Hockin
Portishead, North Somerset

SIR - I used to be a vegan and lost nearly 10lbs; sadly most of it personality.

P.D. Longworth
Overstone, Northamptonshire

Drinking ahead

SIR - We have had various challenges, such as "Dry January" and "Sober October", to raise funds for various charities in recent months.

Let's launch a new campaign to support our local pubs, as they will have suffered through the abstinence months. We could call it Feb-Brewery.

Neil Asher
Loughborough, Leicestershire

SIR - For my contribution to Dry January I have purchased a bottle of non-alcoholic mouthwash.

Dave Alsop
Churchdown, Gloucestershire

SIR - I have purchased a bottle of wine on which is printed: "Perfect with grilled steaks, sausages and burgers. Suitable for vegetarians."

I have not drunk a drop of it yet but already I am feeling confused.

Leonard Macauley
Staining, Lancashire

SIR - The sad fact is that most pubs have become ersatz restaurants.

Many years ago, a noted local poacher used to bring his ferret into the back room of a pub near here and the only objections recorded were from some of the dogs that accompanied most of the customers.

I recall an occasion when, one Saturday morning, some minor media character appeared with a nubile blond girl on each of his arms, and asked the landlady if they could get a ploughman's lunch.

A tractor driver friend of mine observed, not quite *sotto voce*: "Only if you've done a morning ploughing."

Brian Checkland
Thingwall, Wirral

SIR - Terrifically encouraging to read that, according to your Obituaries page, one could be a drinking buddy of Oliver Reed, and somehow still live to 99.

There may be hope for the rest of us yet.

Tom Day
Royston, Hertfordshire

SIR - Having served in the Artists Rifles, my grandfather survived the Great War. He led an active life into his late nineties. I asked him the secret - to which he replied: "Moderation in all things, old boy: stupidest mistake I ever made."

Tony Waldeck
Truro, Cornwall

You're as old as you feel

SIR - News that a Dutchman wants the legal right to knock 20 years off his real age opens up myriad possibilities. I would like to proclaim that I now have a luxuriant, full head of hair. The fact that I have been virtually bald since early adulthood is academic and I shall regard it as a hate crime if people snigger when I brush my imaginary locks.

Peter Forrest
London N6

SIR - I suggested to my wife that she apply for an age increase in order to qualify for her state pension and bus pass. My wounds are only superficial and healing well.

Bob Vass
Bollington, Cheshire

SIR - I downloaded information on how to improve your memory from your article on Saturday and then promptly forgot where I'd put it.

Brian Inns
Melksham, Wiltshire

SIR - As a country cousin I have just spent a rare day travelling in London. Whether on BT rail or the Underground in the crowded carriages, on every occasion I was offered a seat by the young or the not so young.

Are good manners returning - or am I just looking that much older?

Victoria Helstrip
Cranleigh, Surrey

SIR - I read with amusement the idea that we get nicer as we get older.

In fact there is a sort of Laffer curve on this, and at 80 one can move on from being merely difficult to being utterly impossible, capitalising on people saying: "He's wonderful for 80."

R.J.H. Griffiths
Havant, Hampshire

SIR - Any list of contenders for wonders of the modern world must surely include Keith Richards, indestructible member of the Rolling Stones.

Charles Dobson
Burton in Kendal, Cumbria

Flagging in the bagging area

SIR - As I was standing near to some poor unfortunate who was attempting to use a supermarket self-checkout machine, the thing suddenly announced: "Biscuits badly packed in bag." Now that these contraptions can obviously admonish us, and being acutely aware of my own packing abilities, I decided to steer well clear.

Anthony Perrin
Farnham, Surrey

SIR - I was proudly informed by a popular mobile phone store the other day that it was now cashless.

The card machines were down.

George Mascall
Erith, Kent

SIR - Tesco is to open 15 new "low-cost" stores called Jack's.

Too Lidl, too late, if you ask me.

C.J. Adams
Wappenham, Northamptonshire

SIR - I rarely shop in Waitrose owing to the fact that I can feel my fellow shoppers' sense of entitlement.

Simon Warde
Bognor Regis, West Sussex

Dress for the job you have

SIR - As a young police constable working on the Dennis Nilsen case, my husband and his fellow PCs felt they were not always party to the information they were entitled.
To this end they had a tie produced featuring a little mushroom logo: ergo, "Kept in the dark and fed bull---t".

He's thinking of wearing it during the last stage of the Brexit negotiations.

Susy Goodwin
Ware, Hertfordshire

SIR - A former colleague once told me of his father's advice never to trust a man with a bow tie, brown shoes or a beard. Amusingly, his boss at the time sported all three.

Keith Strickland
Trowbridge, Wiltshire

Fewer clothes? No Kon do

SIR - I know that decluttering, as per the advice of tidying guru Marie Kondo, often works to the benefit of the charity shops.

But could there not be some liaison as to areas targeted? We have had three collection bags so far this week. By this time next week we will not have anything to wear.

Richard Woodmore
Hengoed, Glamorgan

SIR - After my father, who proudly boasted never to have owned a pair of jeans, became permanently bedbound I disposed of all his formal clothing in favour of clothes that were easy to dress him in and launder.

So it was that he attended his own funeral dressed in a smart tracksuit - which I like to think astonished my late mother when he bounded athletically up to heaven.

Geraldine Durrant
East Grinstead, West Sussex

SIR - At her request, we buried my twin in her *Game of Thrones* onesie (with its logo "Winter is Coming"). Her bright red Icelandic wool socks were added, to keep her feet warm.

Catherine Shippey
Dorchester, Dorset

SIR - I was so pleased to read that it is now the fashion among the younger generation to leave one's shirt tails hanging out. It even has an official name: a French tuck. As I am six feet six inches tall I have always had a problem with shirts being too short, so that whenever I bend down my shirt tail pops out. Now at the age of 74 I find that I have been a trendsetter for all these years. Even David Beckham follows my lead.

Rod Wells
Cambridge

SIR - I only wish that the Rev Dr Spooner were here to deliver his view of the "French tuck".

Gabriel Lavelle
Chipping Norton, Oxfordshire

The cruellest cut

SIR - The latest "must have" fashion statement is a haircut identical to the one inflicted upon me on the second day of pre-Sandhurst recruit training in the early Seventies, when shoulder-length locks were all the rage.

Nicky Samengo-Turner
Hundon, Suffolk

SIR - I will greatly miss Karl Lagerfeld.

He was an icon, a renaissance man and the only man of his years that was stylish with a ponytail.

Many other men beyond their youth attempt to look good with a ponytail. They cannot. Please desist immediately.

Ralph Herson
London NW1

SIR - Barbers of today benefit from a tendency in men willing to pay for expert husbandry of their beards. I would, however, suggest that the benefit is probably offset by the current fashion for chrome domes - which are often the subject of DIY upkeep.

Doona Turner
Horsham, Surrey

SIR - I'm afraid that all men who are bald or with shaved heads look the same to me. My husband knows to keep a good head of hair.

Jacky Staff
Enniskillen, County Fermanagh

Heads, shoulders, knees and toes

SIR - The modern style of fastening your top button on your shirt collar while not wearing a tie is known as "air tie". Presumably if I don't wear any headwear while I'm out, it is known as an "air hat".

Dave Bassett
Liverpool

SIR It seems that wearers of baseball caps are obliged to keep them on the head at all times, probably even in bed.

Shirley Puckett
Tenterden, Kent

SIR - While visiting a very traditional squash club in the Seventies, a fellow member of my university team wore long, multi-coloured, mis-matched socks on court.

Although his home team opponent was sporting a pair of pink hockey socks, he was nevertheless ridiculed by a team mate's call from the gallery: "I say, Hugo, you're being out-socked!"

Colin Henderson
Cranleigh, Surrey

SIR - I have just lopped off the toes from a number of old socks, and they are now doing great service as insulation for pots of seedlings. My suggestion that the discarded toes might make effective egg cosies, however, was not so readily welcomed.

Andrew Gould
Bradfield, Devon

A helping hand

SIR - When I started work in the Sixties two colleagues were arm amputees, one left and the other right. As and when, they would share a new pair of gloves. That was until they fell out over whose turn it was to pay.

Chris Ainsworth
Newmarket, Suffolk

SIR - I wonder how many acrylic fingernails are sold and subsequently disposed of in landfill every year.

I think most of us are able to grow our own totally recyclable fingernails.

Ian Franklin
Totnes, Devon

SIR – Recycling is not a new thing. I still have a tag from a pair of Marks and Spencers trousers which bears the words: "These trousers are made from 14 recycled plastic bottles".

Mary Calthrop
Whitstable, Kent

The ties that bind

SIR – While returning home on the Underground after watching a day of Test cricket at Lord's, I offered my seat to an elderly lady. She eagerly accepted my offer, saying that I was a gentleman from a gentleman's club (I was wearing an MCC tie).

I am not sure that she realised that the term "gentleman's club" has less salubrious connotations in today's society.

Philip Samengo-Turner
Cirencester, Gloucestershire

SIR – The best hotel in Lincolnshire naturally insists on ties and jackets when dining. However, there is no mention of trousers.

I will take mine just in case.

Keith Wright
Lincoln

SIR – My father wore a tie every working day of his life in case he had to clean a microscope slide with it.

Dr William A. McFadzean
Swansea

SIR – Gently loosening the knot (whether Windsor or other) on a tie is nearly as exciting as undoing buttons on a waistcoat. The more formal the attire, the more rampant the desire. Gentlemen, to abandon the tie is to embrace the prosaic.

Suzette Hill
Ledbury, Herefordshire

A YEAR IN
POLITICS

Honour in defeat

SIR – Though we all appreciate Gareth Southgate's efforts to drag the English football team out of the doldrums, I must question the granting of an OBE. After all, in the World Cup we only made it to the semi-final. What would have been appropriate if we'd won it? King? Sainthood?

Alisdair Low
Richmond, Surrey

SIR – With Michael Palin becoming Sir Michael Palin, he really will be a Knight Who Says Ni.

Joshua Kerr
Kidderminster, Worcestershire

SIR – Is Victoria Caroline Beckham OBE still Posh?

C.J. Fletcher
Stanton St John, Oxfordshire

In nobody's interests

SIR – The two Union Flags behind Bank of England governor Mark Carney at his naturalised British citizenship ceremony were upside-down – much like his past policy on interest rates.

Charles Tweedie
Ludlow, Shropshire

SIR - Going by the latest Treasury forecasts, we have now moved from Project Fear to Project Absolute Terror.

Charlie Whyte
Swadlincote, Derbyshire

SIR - It's not so much his slavish advocacy of Remain - Mr Carney is the man who introduced the appalling plastic banknotes. Sufficient reason to have him deported.

Andrew Dyke
London N21

Notable figures

SIR - I applaud the campaign to put a person of colour on the new £50 note - but unfortunately that will not increase ethnic minority representation in my purse.

Valerie Thompson
Stratford-upon-Avon, Warwickshire

SIR - It occurs to me that I should be the face on the new £50 note for the following reasons:

I do not represent any minority or majority group.

I am neither young or old, wealthy or poor.

My unusual name means I cannot be associated with any particular background.

I am simply an ordinary British woman.

I appreciate that I have not yet died, but then only an insignificant number of the public are even aware of my existence.

I also appreciate that I am not a scientist, let alone a prominent one, but there is still time and if there is one trait the British applaud it is ambition.

Marishelle Butler
East Meon, Hampshire

SIR – Alerted to the fact that my fivers won't biodegrade, I shall now be more careful over their disposal.

Richard Weeks
Felixstowe, Suffolk

Clean up politics

SIR – It has come to my notice that a new super sewer is being constructed underneath the River Thames, passing close to the Houses of Parliament.

Is this not an ideal time to connect it up to the Commons and flush out the detritus that lingers therein?

D.J. Anning
Wendover, Buckinghamshire

SIR – This afternoon I found myself driving behind a large tanker – the sort that empties septic tanks and slurry pits here in rural Devon. Writ large on its sides and rear were the words: "This tank is full of political promises".

Maura Ashworth
Holsworthy, Devon

Party animals

SIR - At least when the BBC positions its reporters outside Downing Street, it gives viewers the opportunity to glimpse the one useful incumbent of the premises: Larry, the Chief Mouser to the Cabinet Office.

Robert Barlow
Smeeth, Kent

SIR - They should replace the Downing Street cat with a Manx cat. They are rudderless.

Roy Hughes
Burntwood, Staffordshire

SIR - Banksy's painting *Devolved Parliament* shows a Commons staffed by chimpanzees. Banksy is being grossly unfair to chimpanzees, who would have done a far superior job compared to the current rabble.

Geoffrey Woolhouse
Moreton-in-Marsh, Gloucestershire

SIR - Amid all the Cabinet appointments, sackings and resignations, there has been no mention of Larry the cat. For the sake of the country, I do hope he has survived the bloodbath.

Michael I. Draper
Nether Wallop, Hampshire

Ticking over nicely

SIR - Westminster is on holiday, along with most political commentators. Amazingly the country still functions and the Brexit debate has almost disappeared. It's marvellous - please could they all have 52 weeks of holiday a year.

Mike Metcalfe
Butleigh Wootton, Somerset

SIR - Don't you just long for the days when John Prescott clutching a Chinese mitten crab in a jar and naming it Peter (after Mandelson) made headline news?

That was August 1997, when all we had to worry about was who was "minding the shop" while Tony Blair was on holiday.

Gill Downs
Folkestone, Kent

SIR - Many were grateful for the holiday from the Brexit debate over Christmas and New Year but, suffering from withdrawal symptoms, I found a bottle of Chateau Corbin, a St Emilion. An improvement on the other Corbyn, we were cheered and ready for another week.

John Main
Sleaford, Lincolnshire

Speaker's corner

SIR - You report that a shadow minister with a mild Geordie accent has claimed £250 for voice coaching lessons.

I trust that the money was well spent, and that he now has a proper Geordie accent.

David Brown
Lavenham, Suffolk

SIR - For many centuries there has been a parliamentary convention whereby, upon his or her appointment, the Speaker is dragged to the chair.

Since the present incumbent, by his words and deeds, seeks to introduce "innovation", may I suggest one that might prove popular? Namely, when he develops a god complex, to permit MPs to have him dragged from it.

Roger Hitt
Kenley, Surrey

SIR - Does anyone know where I could get a "D--- -s to Bercow" sticker for my car?

Karl Williams
Glasgow

SIR - Have pity on poor Mr Bercow; after all, he's no Betty Boothroyd.

S. Shepherd
High Wycombe, Buckinghamshire

TIG-ger warning

SIR - It has been suggested that The Independent Group should be termed TIG. How about expanding the acronym to TIGGER - or The Independent Group of Groaning

Europhile Remainers, to give them their full bounceability.

Richard W. Turner
Nazeing, Essex

SIR – As The Independent Group are avowed advocates of a further people's referendum, would it not be apt to rename it "The People's Independent Group"?

The resulting acronym would also be easier to remember.

Roger Hobson
Market Harborough, Leicestershire

SIR – With all the comings and goings at Westminster recently, will there be enough room on the ballot paper at the next general election to cater for all parties?

Lawrence Gordon
Sutton Coldfield

Friends or foe?

SIR – No need for rebel MP Anna Soubry to work too hard to achieve her ambition of destroying the Conservative Party.

By thwarting a no-deal Brexit the Tories appear to be quite capable of doing it themselves.

Christopher Gill
Aberdyfi, Gwynedd

SIR - Can whoever leaves the Conservative party last please turn off the lights.

Peter Wiltshire
Binfield, Berkshire

SIR - So much for the EU credentials of the three breakaway Conservative MPs, erroneously self-styled as the three amigos.

If they knew any European languages at all then they would be the three amigas.

Daphne Silvester
London N6

SIR - Would the turncoat MPs from both sides of the House please stop calling for me: I am currently far too busy internationally.

Unity Lawler
Heysham, Lancashire

Grayling runs aground

SIR - Following the collapse of the government's deal with Seaborne Freight, a ferry firm with no ferries to its name, I am contemplating registering a new start-up company - Seaborneyesterday Freight Ltd.

The company would specialise in providing ferries in the event of a no-deal Brexit.

I will make a proposition to Chris Grayling, the Transport Secretary, to provide 50 non-existent ferries for £1 million - a saving of £13 million on the previous failed deal.

If required, I would be prepared to increase this number to 100 non-existent ferries - at no additional cost.

Peter Kievenaar
Chelsworth, Suffolk

SIR - Christopher Grayling has been responsible for a catalogue of errors that have caused misery and hardship.

As he was born on April Fool's Day, he should be appointed Secretary of State for the Ministry of Silly Walks and allowed to keep his salary of over £140,000.

Gary Williamson
Kingston upon Thames, Surrey

SIR - Chris Grayling confirmed as Minister for Brewery Visits?

Anne Coward
Banstead, Surrey

Leaving herself defenceless

SIR - Theresa May does not just shoot herself in the foot. She does it methodically toe by toe, both feet in almost daily succession.

To sack Defence Secretary Gavin Williamson in such a manner, on the eve of a local election, must be genius self-destruction.

Howard K. Ford
Tadworth, Surrey

SIR - One good reason why Mr Williamson had to go was that he always referred to our navy ships as Haitch MS this and Haitch MS that.

David Tingle
Codicote, Hertfordshire

SIR - I am surprised that Mrs May did not give the job of Defence Secretary to her new buddy Jeremy Corbyn. This would have been a decision of similar quality to many of her recent decisions.

Roger Boyce
Romsey, Hampshire

Chinese whispers

SIR - I have today learnt, for the first time, how one should pronounce the name of the Chinese telecoms giant Huawei.

Having grown up on the banks of the Tyne, I had previously translated it into the Geordie "Ha'way".

I am much relieved to find that it is not a Geordie concern.

John Golightly
Torrington, Devon

SIR - The only sensible thing Theresa May has done recently is to allow Huawei to take over our communications network. If they want to listen in to my telephone conversations, they will at least have to provide a more comprehensive network in Devon.

R. MacDonnell
London SW15

Yes ministers

SIR – Whatever happened to those nodding dogs we used to see through the rear window in cars?

I was reminded of them today watching the BBC's footage of Mrs May addressing the Cabinet.

Wendy Breese
Lingfield, Surrey

SIR – Why do Cabinet ministers walk down Downing Street clutching mugs of coffee? I thought austerity was over. Surely Number 10 can afford to serve coffee and biscuits at Cabinet meetings.

W.K. Wood
Bolton, Lancashire

SIR – If the government is going to ban the use of straws in the interests of reducing plastic waste, what will ministers have left to clutch at?

Dag Pike
Bristol

SIR – I am feeling increasingly inadequate and unknowledgable: as yet another Tory minister resigns, I wonder who most of them are and what they actually did.

Tony Parrack
London SW20

Electorate all at sea

SIR - We may now be in uncharted territory but rarely, if ever, can a crew have been so disgusted with the efforts of those on the bridge.

If an election were called, it would be like being asked to choose between a heart attack or a stroke.

> **John Stewart**
> Terrick, Buckinghamshire

SIR - I am a lifelong Conservative-voting Manchester United supporter - so imagine my emotions at present.

> **Stewart French**
> Ashford, Kent

SIR - In order to restore trust in our political system, the time has surely come for us to replace most of our MPs with 600 estate agents.

> **Jeremy Brittain-Long**
> Falmouth, Cornwall

SIR - If a comedian with no political experience can be elected president of Ukraine, who could stand for the next prime minister of this country?

Although not strictly a comedian, I nominate Rory Bremner. After all, he could do all the voices of the Cabinet members.

> **Cynthia Denby**
> Edgware, Middlesex

SIR - I am concerned that the Conservative Party's vice-chairman for policy is a Mr Skidmore.

While we would hope that we shouldn't be overly worried about nominative determinism, memories emerge of a Mr Reckless – who was found legless in the lobby and departed for Ukip.

Juliet Henderson
South Warnborough, Hampshire

SIR – Can we now hold a vote of no competence: no competence, that is, in the whole of the political class.

It's a good job they are not paid on the basis of their productivity.

David Crawford
Llandudno, Conwy

Vote early, vote often

SIR – I have voted in 15 general elections since 1964 and have yet to vote for the winning candidate, despite living in a wide variety of constituencies from the Home Counties to the North East.

I have every confidence that at the next election I will again cast my vote for a loser.

If any readers consider that this ability is worth financial reward, I look forward to hearing from them.

Andy Trask
Haslemere, Surrey

SIR – My first experience of voting was in a mock election at the Royal Liberty School, Romford, held to coincide with the 1955 general election. All the major parties fielded candidates who canvassed for votes and held meetings.

My vote went to the runaway winner: The Yeti Nationalist.
Oh, that my choice could be made so easily these days.

William Pease
Southam, Warwickshire

SIR - When I worked in the Commons I took a schoolboyish
delight in sneaking along forbidden corridors and being in
places where I was not allowed. However, I paid the price.
Once I entered a "Members only" lift. At the next level I
was horrified when Enoch Powell, that great stickler for the
rules, stepped in. He stared long and hard at the "Members
only" notice, and then stared long and hard at me, before
commenting: "Oh dear, I must have missed the by-election."

Chris Moncrieff
Woodford Green, Essex

Taking over the asylum

SIR - The whole political class is a disgrace. I shall vote
Monster Raving Loony next time. See if I don't.

Bob Payne
Hythe, Hampshire

SIR - From now on, I will use my Grand National
method to determine how I will cast my vote for the next
parliamentary elections. This entails a list of runners,
closed eyes and a pin.

Keith Harrison
Morpeth, Northumberland

SIR - My husband has been saying for years that he would like to form a new political party. He would call it The Common Sense and Logic Party.

All our friends say they would vote for it.

Elspeth Tagg
Tadworth, Surrey

SIR - I'm fairly adept at operating a credit card, I understand the meaning of the word "democracy", I don't need a duck house, I abhor Marxism and am a reasonably "honourable member" of society. Any jobs going?

Cameron Morice
Reading, Berkshire

Stormy times for the Lib Dems

SIR - The Liberal Democrats seem to want to change the electorate to suit their views, rather than reflect the views of their electorate. It is as sensible as seeking to change the sea to suit a type of ship.

Andrew Wauchope
London SE11

SIR - Apart from being a convenient repository for wasted votes, what is the point of the Liberal Democrats?

Jo Bird
Slapton, Devon

SIR - By the logic of the Liberals Democrats' attitude to the referendum result, their new leader should not be Jo

Swinson but Ed Davey — because he lost.

Rev Philip Harratt
Montgomery, Powys

Sir Nick's new friends

SIR - I would like to ask Sir Nick Clegg (with apologies
to Mrs Merton) what it was that first attracted him to the
£1 million-a-year job with Facebook.

John Curran
Bristol

SIR - Politically idle minds will miss Nick Clegg. Whatever
he said, one was safe taking the opposite view. There's no
one equally dependable.

Andrew Rayner
Wadebridge, Cornwall

SIR - After "serving" the public, Tony Blair has had the
nous to create a large business enterprise and to be sought
after. Nick Clegg has been thought to have brains enough to
be employable.

David Cameron is bored.

What does that say about how he is perceived by
politicians, entrepreneurs and his fellow citizens?

Dr Richard A.E. Grove
Isle of Whithorn, Wigtownshire

Labour veers leftwards

SIR - When Jeremy Corbyn was filmed leaving his house by ITV, it was reassuring to see him remain loyal to his socialist principles.

The road sign at the end of the street clearly indicated that it was a right-turn only junction; but Mr Corbyn was not deterred and confidently cycled left.

Mr A.B. Cowling
Epsom, Surrey

SIR - One of my father's favourite expressions was "I blame the Labour government".

This was regardless of which party was in power.

Dr P.E. Pears
Coleshill, Warwickshire

SIR - I have noticed a worrying spike in my daily blood pressure readings lately. This can be no coincidence in the week of the Labour Party conference.

Michael Withers
Lytham St Annes, Lancashire

SIR - My labrador was recently given a pack of three balls: red, yellow and blue. The yellow one she tossed into the long grass next door; the blue one she reduced to an unrecognisable pulp.

She seems to like the red one. I hope this is not a warning of dreadful things to come.

Lesley Ballard
Sevenoaks, Kent

Oh, Jeremy Corbyn

SIR – If there is anything to be admired in Jeremy Corbyn, it is the fact that he is not Tony Blair: a sentiment that is likely to be approved of, albeit for different reasons, over the whole political spectrum.

Robert Arnold
Southend-on-Sea, Essex

SIR – While penning a letter to you about the Labour leader, I typed "Corbyn" and my spellcheck offered me three options: Ignore, Ignore All or Add.

I took the first option and would recommend this to others.

Dr Ken Garrett
Leeds, West Yorkshire

SIR – I am not so much concerned about the ingredients of Jeremy Corbyn's pie but whether our sky is big enough.

J. Eric Nolan
Wilpshire, Lancashire

SIR – Congratulations to Con Coughlin on using the words "Corbyn" and "intelligence" in the same sentence.

David Bucker
London NW11

SIR – With apologies to typesetters at the *Guardian*, Jeremy Corbyn's Labour is a cult.

Charles Foster
Chalfont St Peter, Buckinghamshire

SIR - My father-in-law was helped by his parents in making dress code judgments by being given a symbolic gold pistol to hang off his watch chain with which to "shoot himself" if he were ever to appear at an occasion inappropriately dressed. Perhaps something for Mr Corbyn's Christmas list?

Charles Holden
Micheldever, Hampshire

SIR - I see that Jeremy Corbyn is once again described as looking like "a scruffy geography teacher". I'm starting to resent it. My husband was a geography teacher for 35 years and has never looked scruffy at work.

Dianne Fielding
Halifax, West Yorkshire

SIR - Michael Foot: Mr Corbyn's political and sartorial role model.

Frank Lee
Dronfield, Derbyshire

McDonnell does the maths

SIR - Why on earth is anyone criticising John McDonnell for saying he will not use 11 Downing Street as his home when he becomes Chancellor of the Exchequer?

Mrs May has obviously decided to hand Jeremy Corbyn the next election on a plate, so surely it is only sensible to plan for the future.

Andrew Rixon
Hertford

SIR - When asked to give a one-word answer to the question whether Winston Churchill was a hero or a villain, John McDonnell said "Tonypandy - villain".

Given that the number of words he used was double the number requested, there must surely be some concern about the economy's prospects were Mr McDonnell ever to be appointed Chancellor.

> **Richard Lewis**
> London N1

SIR - If Jeremy Corbyn truly wants to understand the British sense of irony, he need look no further than your headline: "Labour will open the door to anyone with a skill [says] Diane Abbott".

> **Philip Crowe**
> Sheffield

Stone cold broke

SIR - I do hope the crumbling doorstep and flaky paintwork of No 11, shown on the front page of your Budget special supplement, are not indicative of the country's finances.

> **John Harvey**
> Haslemere, Surrey

SIR - I always told our children that the money tree was deciduous. I shall be very surprised if the Chancellor's is any different.

> **Geoff Cullington**
> Dorchester

SIR – What is the definition of austerity these days – only one car per family?

Tony Lawson
Slough, Berkshire

May is MIA

SIR – Could everyone please check behind their sofas? The Prime Minister seems to have gone missing.

James Farrington
Hartfield, East Sussex

SIR – The ability to face both ways at once might be a useful attribute for a contortionist or circus performer. It is undesirable in a prime minister.

Dr Catherine Moloney
Liverpool

SIR – Mrs May simply does not listen. I assume that if she ever goes into hospital the board above her bed will say "Nil by Ear".

Frederick Hill
Chipping Norton, Oxfordshire

SIR – The initials of the greatest woman prime minister since the war are TM – "but not necessarily in the right order".

Paul Winterburn
Trowbridge, Wiltshire

Digging in her kitten heels

SIR - I once owned a machine called an autoscythe. If you hit a solid object before de-clutching, it simply started to dig itself into the ground - which it continued to do, clutch locked, until you disconnected the plug lead.

Theresa May reminds me of it.

Mark Miller
Humbie, East Lothian

SIR - Mrs May is like the guest who doesn't know when it's time to leave the party. You put on your pyjamas, switch off the lights and in the morning she is still sitting on the sofa.

Joan Campanini Russell
Twickenham, Middlesex

SIR - The more obdurate Mrs May becomes, the thicker and brighter her lipstick.

Pamela Lunn
Faringdon, Oxfordshire

SIR - The Americans have an acronym for the President Of The United States: POTUS.

I suggest one for Theresa May - First Lord Of the Treasury Supported by A Minority: FLOTSAM.

Paul Anglesea
Wrexham, Denbighshire

SIR - The Prime Minister has invoked the example of her hero Geoff Boycott as she stays at the crease. However, in a famous Test Match many years ago Mr Boycott was left on his own on 99 not out as all the other England batsmen were dismissed. Mrs May seems to be heading for the same fate.

Geoff Blackman
Mullion, Cornwall

SIR – We have renamed our cat Theresa. She keeps saying she wants to go out, but when we open the door she dithers half-in and half-out before eventually remaining in.

Richard Verschoyle
Okehampton, Devon

SIR – The period of civil wars between Stephen and Matilda (1135-54) is known as the Anarchy. Will the terribly divisive three years over which Theresa May has presided one day be called the Uncertainty?

Mary Lanch
Harrow, Middlesex

SIR – I may be the only person in these islands who wishes Mrs May to stay on as Prime Minister.

After 50 years of marriage to a Yorkshire girl, this is the first time she has admitted to me that someone's utterances have left her "speechless". May it continue.

David Evans
Wilmslow, Cheshire

Boris on manoeuvres

SIR – I propose our dancing Prime Minister doesn't waste another minute of these crucial Brexit talks and cuts straight to the chase with a *Strictly Brexit* dance-off. Both she and Boris have been desperate to grasp the centre stage, both taking great measures to get the right posture, yet we all know the performance is a lot of arm-flapping, and little direction.

Tim Worley
Dorking, Surrey

SIR - Kenneth Clarke says that Boris Johnson could not run a whelk stall. But Boris would appoint the best person to run the whelk stall and then leave him or her to get on with the job - something beyond the capability of any recent prime minister.

Antony Dew
London SW13

SIR - If Boris Johnson is the solution then the diagnosis is assuredly wrong.

Frank Sloan
Rochester, Kent

SIR - I see it is the intention to take Boris Johnson to court over possible fibbing. This could lead to a rapid depletion in the number of MPs sitting in the House of Commons.

Godfrey Brangham
Usk, Monmouthshire

SIR - On discovering the full name Alexander Boris de Pfeffel Johnson, I laughed: "How appropriate! Exactly describes the man!"

I then realised I had misread his name; it wasn't Piffle after all, but Pfeffel. Close enough though.

Christine Davidson
Chichester, West Sussex

SIR - Boris Johnson appears to be taming his locks; a slightly more svelte look for a possible leadership challenge, perhaps? However, we shall know that the game is really afoot when Jacob Rees-Mogg is seen in a single-breasted suit.

Tim Lovett
Claygate, Surrey

SIR - With Boris Johnson in Number 10, a new Churchillian era dawns.
    Memo to self: reinstate the Anderson shelter; restock with tins of Spam and French brandy.

Trelawney Ffrench
Ascot, Berkshire

SIR - Can someone please tell Boris Johnson to buy a tin of shoe polish.

Frank Ryan
Burnham-on-Sea, Somerset

SIR - One of the best things about Boris Johnson being elected Prime Minister is watching the BBC's Laura Kuenssberg enunciate his name through clenched teeth.

Andy Ritchie
Loxwood, West Sussex

SIR - I applaud the Prime Minister's commitment to recruit 20,000 additional police officers – but wouldn't it be cheaper and more effective just to get the Attorney General Geoffrey Cox to narrate the Ten Commandments against a background track of rolling thunder?

Wrong 'uns and ne'er-do-wells would surely repent by the busload under the magnificent reverberations of that voice.

Neil Truelove
Clifton, Bedfordshire

SIR – No Fox. No Hunt. Tally-ho!

Mary Whitehead
Hove, East Sussex

The old guard

SIR – Jacob Rees-Mogg must be a modern wonder. He can be the only living creature from the 19th century still alive and active in the 21st (apart from tortoises in the Galapagos Islands).

Tony Palmer
Hope Valley, Derbyshire

SIR – Upon searching for "Jacob Rees-Mogg" using *The Daily Telegraph*'s web search facility, the first hits were: "Buy Jacob Rees-Mogg at Amazon" and "Jacob Rees-Mogg: buy handmade or vintage items from the most vibrant online marketplace".

It's bad enough that the poor chap has been sold out by his party leader, but is Mrs May selling him off now too?

Chris Tyrrell
London E1

A Tory Labours in vain

SIR - Jacob Rees-Mogg, in his botched attempt to get Mrs May out of Downing Street, fell pitifully short of the success of his late father William, in his capacity of Editor of *The Times*, in getting Mick Jagger out of jail.

Stephen Wallis
Billericay, Essex

SIR - A timely new job opportunity has arisen for Jacob Rees-Mogg - Nanny to his sister's children when she takes up her seat in Brussels.

Amanda Karpinski
Shepton Mallet, Somerset

SIR - It seems rather unfortunate that Jacob Rees-Mogg should have chosen ERG as the name for his lobby group. The erg (sic) is also a very small unit of work in the centimetre/gram/second of measurements.

M.G. Walker
Chippenham, Wiltshire

Headed for the cliff edge

SIR - I believe the Conservatives need a new party logo. I suggest a lemming.

Richard Billington
Guildford, Surrey

SIR - The Conservative Party is suffering from electile dysfunction - the inability to arouse the electorate.

The same could be said of Labour and other parties.

W.M. Barraclough
Swilland, Suffolk

SIR - I do wish that politicians could be swapped like footballers. We could have Kate Hoey in the side and sell on Ken Clarke.

Dr Alistair A. Donald
Watlington, Oxfordshire

SIR - As a traditional Tory voter, I have only one thing to say: bring back David Miliband.

Sue Campbell
London SW6

It's my party, and I'll leave if I want to

SIR - I cancelled my membership of the Conservative Party because I am appalled by their incompetence in government.

That said, I am so furious that I will probably join again simply for the pleasure of leaving again.

Steve Anderson
Brentwood, Essex

SIR - I received a communication from the Conservative Party this morning containing three books of raffle tickets. As they sped towards the bin, I paused to wonder whether, given the haemorrhaging of members from the party, I would find that the odds on my winning the top prize had greatly shortened were I to abandon the habit of a lifetime and send them in.

Gregory P. Morris
Penymynydd, Flintshire

SIR - A large number of ordinary working men in my town are members of the local Conservative Association, despite the other two leading parties having their headquarters nearby.

When I asked a long-standing member whether this was due to a possible leadership contest, he replied: "No, it's because we have the best snooker tables."

David Ainsworth
Manchester

Bloody difficult woman

SIR - How, in a country famous around the world for its redoubtable matrons - usually clad in bullet-proof tweed, and never taking no for an answer - did we find Theresa May in charge?

Lucy Beney
Charlton Horethorne, Somerset

SIR - If she had the slightest degree of self-awareness, she would change her name by deed poll from May to Can't.

Nick Brigham
Hexham, Northumberland

SIR - Mrs May exhorts us to hold our nerve with regard to

her latest Brexit deal.

Me, I'm holding my nose.

Dr D.A. Moore
Colchester, Essex

SIR - Brexit is now a Gordian knot. What we need is
someone with a large sharp sword. Instead, we have Theresa
May with a pair of nail scissors.

A.H. Peake
Barnstaple, North Devon

SIR - You are in hospital for a minor ailment.

The surgeon comes round to see you and wants you to
agree to have your perfectly good leg amputated. Naturally
you refuse.

He comes round on the second day with the same
request, that you agree to have your leg amputated. You
reply: "Look, I've told you once, now please f--- off."

The third day he comes round and says, "Look, let me cut
your leg off and I promise I will retire directly afterwards."

Alan Stedall
Sutton Coldfield

SIR - A quiz question surely for the future:
"In what year was the end of May in June?"

Wayne Hickman
Loughton, Essex

SIR - Now that we are to have a new prime minister,
perhaps the country could unite in one resolve: the kissing
has to stop.

Let our new leader stride onto the international stage with an open countenance and an outstretched arm ready with a good old British handshake. Then we can begin to take pride in our way of life again.

M. Erskine
Cupar, Fife

Leading question

SIR - I browse the shelf of yellow and black books in my local store from time to time, and have noticed that "Tory Leadership for Dummies" is missing. Has the title been withdrawn, or has it simply sold out?

Andrew Bond
Wells, Somerset

SIR - It is interesting for students of politics to witness Conservative MPs competing furiously to be Leader of the Opposition.

John Catchpole
Beverley, East Yorkshire

SIR - Hopefully by deciding not to attend Channel 4's leadership debate, Boris Johnson has started a new approach to these political programmes. I look forward to all the lecterns being unoccupied in future.

Richard Tweed
Croydon, Surrey

SIR - After the much heralded BBC "debate" between our aspiring prime ministers it occurs to me that the BBC could well stand for the Boris Baiting Consortium.

Cdr David Hopkinson RN (retd)
St Just-in-Roseland, Cornwall

SIR - What bad luck for Boris that he is a British politician at the mercy of our sanctimonious media rather than a French politician - for whom, judging by the personal behaviour of recent leaders, anything goes.

Mary Robinson
Mansfield, Nottinghamshire

SIR - I cannot begin to tell you how heartened I am to see the state of Boris Johnson's car.

Finally, a candidate with a life - dirty clothes, coffee cups and, rather delightfully, a Tintin book in French.

Forget prime minister. Boris for king.

Susy Goodwin
Ware, Hertfordshire

SIR - Michael Gove is happy to delay Brexit until 2020. It just goes to show: never trust anyone who goes jogging wearing black ankle socks.

Chris Barmby
Tonbridge, Kent

SIR - My wife suggests that I should put my name forward for the Tory Party leadership. No one has heard of me, but that doesn't appear to be a disadvantage.

Adrian Fyles
Blackburn, Lancashire

High hopes

SIR - The disclosure by Tory MP Rory Stewart that he has smoked opium makes his proposal for a Citizens' Assembly very slightly more understandable.

Carey Waite
Lewes, East Sussex

SIR - According to archaeologists, people in western China 2,500 years ago may have smoked cannabis to communicate with the dead. In their youth, were some Conservative Party leadership candidates merely trying to reconnect with the spirit of Winston Churchill?

Richard George
St Albans, Hertfordshire

SIR - Although I'm no fan of Michael Gove, his distant past cocaine use is fairly low on my list of reasons. If the Conservatives are looking for a leader with an unblemished past personal life, we could end up with another Theresa May.

Jacqueline Statham
Cheltenham, Gloucestershire

SIR - *Twas brillig and the slithy Goves*
  Did gyre and gimble in the wabe;

You have to wonder what they were on.

Andrew Dane
York

SIR – I may be in the running for a job as a school crossings warden. Because of this I would like to publicly confess that 70 years ago, when I was only 13 years old and didn't know any better, I scrumped apples from my local vicarage's orchard. I most sincerely apologise for this.

Keith Garner
Scunthorpe, Lincolnshire

SIR – I wonder if Michael Gove need worry about getting a visa to enter the US, given his admission of past drug use.

When I was young and believed that a stupid question on a visa application form merited a stupid answer, I replied to the question "Do you intend to overthrow the federal government by force or violence?" by writing "violence". I was granted a visa without demur.

Ron Forrest
Wells, Somerset

Two political heavyweights

SIR – Boris Johnson should put some weight back on. Shakespeare always knew what he was talking about. He made Julius Caesar say (Act I, Scene 2): "Let me have about me men that are fat... Yond Cassius (Hunt) has a lean and hungry look. He thinks too much; such men are dangerous."

Shirley Puckett
Tenterden, Kent

SIR - It will be strange indeed if our two largest political parties are simultaneously led by a Jeremy who owed his position on the membership ballot to tactical voting by MPs who never expected him to emerge victorious from the contest.

Laurence Smith
Brimpton Common, Berkshire

SIR - Jeremy Hunt complains that many of his critics deliberately mispronounce his last name.
I assume he is relieved he wasn't christened Isaac.

Richard Scrivener
Colchester, Essex

SIR - Many years ago I had a work colleague called Frank Hunt; and if you valued your teeth, you never called him Fran.
Recent "accidental" corruptions of Jeremy Hunt's name are, like Morecambe and Wise's ad libs, carefully rehearsed.

Ron Mason
East Grinstead, West Sussex

The People have spoken

SIR - It might be interesting to know just who supporters of the campaign for a "People's Vote" on our withdrawal from the EU think voted in the 2016 referendum – dogs, cats, guinea pigs?

Celia Tooth
Halesowen, West Midlands

SIR – There seems to be growing demand in some quarters for a second referendum. I wonder what the choices would be?

Tick one box only:
1. I would choose the current deal.
2. I would choose the Chequers deal.
3. I would choose the Norway deal.
4. I would choose the Canada deal.
5. I would choose a WTO deal.
6. I would choose Boris's deal.
7. I would choose Jeremy Corbyn's deal (whatever that is).
8. I would choose no deal.
9. I would choose to remain in the EU.
10. I would choose to abide by the democratic decision of the previous referendum, but on UK terms.
11. None of the above.
12. Other (specify).

Marilyn Parrott
Altrincham, Cheshire

SIR – At a dinner party over Easter, we used pieces of cutlery to represent all the differing views among MPs over Brexit. We ended up with eight pieces – which illustrates what a meal they are making of it.

Anthony Haslam
Farnham, Surrey

SIR - Brexit seems to have turned into the small print of an advertisement: terms and conditions apply; not available in Northern Ireland.

Dr Bob Turvey
Bristol

SIR - Second referendum?
   Weeks of Nigel Farage.
   No thank you.

Keith Rowlands
Cotheridge, Worcestershire

The dreaded B-word

SIR - The Liberal Democrats are seriously behind the times with their masculine-biased slogan, "B------s to Brexit".
   Government guidelines now recommend gender-neutral or more feminine language. Perhaps "Brexit Is Bust" would have been more appropriate.

Graham Masterton
Tadworth, Surrey

SIR - Our local shop has installed the equivalent of a swear box. Any customer mentioning the word *Brexit* is invited to put a cash forfeit in the box. The shop is run by a relatively young couple but they are already talking about early retirement.

Nairn Lawson
Portbury, Somerset

Boldly going nowhere

SIR - It occurs to me that Brexit is remarkably similar to space travel. Putting it on one's wishlist requires no personal effort or knowledge. Actually achieving it is another kettle of fish.

Raymond Boyland
Worcester

SIR - Sir Keir Starmer is right to offer a second referendum on the Brexit issue if Labour wins a general election. We will need to be a member of the EU in order to be bailed out when Labour bankrupts the country.

Stephen Swindells
Ripon, North Yorkshire

SIR - Sir Keir Starmer has said that the government must have flexible red lines in the withdrawal terms. I reckon that should get us an outcome that is mostly unique and slightly dead.

A. Bazely
Croydon, Surrey

SIR - Uri Geller has threatened to use telepathy to stop Brexit. Unfortunately, his psychic powers appear to be working spontaneously.

James Thacker
Tanworth-in-Arden, Warwickshire

Running out of puff

SIR - Frontogenesis: A word that neatly describes the Brexit talks. A meeting of two different (hot) air currents to form a cloud.

Terence Trelawny Gower
Lowestoft, Suffolk

SIR - I would point out that WTF doesn't just stand for World Trade Federation. It also represents the reaction of a large proportion of the electorate to recent disclosures about the conduct of Brexit negotiations.

Alisdair Low
Richmond, Surrey

SIR - "Sex is a messy business, and if it's not messy then you aren't doing it right."
Maybe the same applies to Brexit negotiations.

Geoffrey Lowndes
Salisbury, Wiltshire

SIR - David Cameron, the man who opened the can.
Theresa May, the woman who kicked it down the road.
Will someone please come forward who can effectively re-seal it or send it to recycling, while avoiding a meltdown?
We want to get on with our lives.

Trevor Lucey
Berkhamsted, Hertfordshire

Brexhausted? Join the club

SIR – Theresa May's Brexit proposal is ridiculous. You don't leave a club by taking out a lifetime subscription.

> **David Paul**
> Leeds, West Yorkshire

SIR – I'm sure most people, including me, have found themselves, at some time, up the creek without a paddle.

But how many of us have deliberately paddled up the creek and then thrown away the paddle?

> **Steve Anderson**
> Brentwood, Essex

SIR – Surely the Brexit conundrum is the Schleswig-Holstein question of our day, but with the twist that the one person who understands it, Laura Kuenssberg, appears to have perfect recall. The rest of us either wish we were dead, or are in the process of going mad.

> **Jane Moth**
> Snettisham, Norfolk

The end of the affair

SIR – Shortly, we'll be able to divorce our spouses without allocating any blame.

Can our politicians learn a lesson here regarding Brexit?

> **Nigel Lines**
> Ringwood, Hampshire

SIR – When my sister got divorced nearly 40 years ago, her then husband demanded "£5,000 and the car owned by our parents". When we finished laughing, he was told he was getting nothing as he was owed nothing. Presumably, Mrs May would have paid him the money, given him the car, filled the tank with petrol and allowed him to send us, and our descendants, any inconvenient bills in perpetuity.

Andrew Thomas
Malvern, Worcestershire

SIR – *Brino* (Brexit in name only) is a fairly good acronym for the government's current plan for leaving the EU. However, I prefer *Lino* (leaving in name only) – our nation is, after all, being walked all over.

David Fouracre
Napton on the Hill, Warwickshire

SIR – Isn't it time that Theresa and Philip May started house hunting on the Continent? She has spent so much time there and appears to have made many new acquaintances.

Andrea O'Donnell
Oxton, Nottinghamshire

SIR – I wonder if Mrs May will get a pension from the EU. She has certainly earned one.

Ian Stewart Mather
Burton upon Trent, Staffordshire

Britain's bottom line

SIR - We see the 500-plus pages of the Brexit deal being waved about in public. I suggest that the A4 pages could be of greater use if ripped to a quarter of their size, and employed by everyone regardless of their standpoint on Europe. Or is the paper inadequately flushable?

Tim Bradbury
Northwich, Cheshire

SIR - Those who do not wish to wade through the 500-page deal will find it is easily shortened to "Sic transit gloria mundi".

Alastair Prain
London SW9

SIR - Given the frustration felt by so many at the proceedings at Westminster, perhaps it might be possible to provide some nationwide entertainment by having the initiator of all this nonsense, David Cameron, hauled around the country in a tumbrel.

Iain Reid
Henley-on-Thames, Oxfordshire

SIR - I have been stranded on a desert island for 13 years and need to catch up on the news; the last thing I saw was David Cameron tell the Conservative Party that they "need to stop banging on about Europe". How has that gone?

Andrew Jukes
Eye, Suffolk

The Commons ground

SIR - In 1241, ten Cardinals attempted to select a successor to Pope Gregory IX. They could not agree. The dictator of Rome, Matteo Rosso Orsini, helped them reach a conclusion. They were shut inside a crumbling building, subject to squalid conditions and harsh treatment. They were denied food and eventually the roof of their debating chamber was removed, exposing them to the elements. Worn down by illness and death, after 60 days they elected Celestine IV.

Could this be a model for achieving Brexit consensus in the Commons?

Bryan Robinson
Worthing, West Sussex

SIR - I've changed horse midstream and now a confirmed Remainer, as this feckless government is totally incapable of running anything.

Valda Mossman
Penzance, Cornwall

SIR - I am in a state of permanent perplexity regarding those members of the electorate who chose to vote for us to leave the EU. Do you seriously mean to tell me that they trusted both British and European politicians to deliver a Brexit which was intended to benefit us?

Patricia Eastwood
Skipton, North Yorkshire

SIR - Congratulations to Mrs May's Brexit adviser, Olly Robbins. He has followed her orders to the letter and should clearly be promoted.

I suggest Ambassador to Outer Mongolia, or further, immediately and permanently.

Vaughan Matthews
Monmouth

SIR – *One elderly statesman with gout*
When asked what Brexit was about
In a written reply
Said, "My colleagues and I
Are doing our best to find out".

John Tilsiter
Radlett, Hertfordshire

Not for turning

SIR – The best way out of the Brexit impasse would be to hand over negotiations to Baroness Thatcher.

I am perfectly aware that the lady has died, but she could still do a better job than the present bunch of incompetents.

Richard Barrett
Halesworth, Suffolk

SIR – Noel Edmonds is the obvious choice to sort this whole fiasco out, given his wealth of experience on the question of *Deal or No Deal*.

Fiona Roberts
Oswestry, Shropshire

SIR - Over the past 12 months I have read credible solutions to most of the prevailing issues, including some very pertinent and profound offerings on Brexit. Surely the way forward is to recruit a cross-section of letter-writers to Mrs May's advisory team. I'm sure there would be no shortage of willing volunteers.

Wg Cdr F.K. Dowling (retd)
Lincoln

Salad days behind us

SIR - Jim Winship, from the British Sandwich Association (really?), threatens a shortage of lettuce if we have a no-deal Brexit.

If so, bravo. Lettuce must be the most boring leaf ever to be persuaded to grow. From now on I will gladly sacrifice my salad garnish for those whose need for this tasteless bit of greenery is obviously greater than mine.

Myra Spalton
Macclesfield, Cheshire

SIR - We are vegetarians and are concerned that under a no-deal Brexit there might be illegal courgettes and tomatoes at risk while trying to cross the Channel in open boats.

We would ask the customs men along the coast to be considerate when making arrests.

K.A. and R.H. Rouse
Sunningdale, Berkshire

SIR - After the humiliation of the Brexit process, I welcome the signs of some rational thinking. I refer to the news that Magnum ice-creams are to be stockpiled. These isles can come through!

John Bastow
Windsor, Berkshire

SIR - Any day now, I am expecting us all to receive an official pamphlet from Downing St on how to reconstruct Noah's Ark in the event of "no deal".

Richard Rouse
Ascot, Berkshire

SIR - Queuing in my local shop to collect my *Daily Telegraph*, I stepped aside to give an elderly, partially sighted lady with a walking stick enough room to turn around and leave. As I did this, the woman behind me immediately pushed past me to be served.

Is this an example of the type of civil unrest we can expect after Brexit?

Shirley Batten-Smith
Watford, Hertfordshire

SIR - Sir Vince Cable's suggestion that Brexit could ruin *Strictly* is just another excellent reason to leave.

Tony Fricker
Haywards Heath, West Sussex

SIR - The latest Brexit scare - namely the potential shortage of sperm - is surely a rallying cry to all young British men who voted for Brexit to rise up and take matters into their own hands.

Malcolm Bransgrove
West Wittering, West Sussex

Drama in Europe

SIR - The British side could offer a sweetener to the EU's chief negotiator, Michel Barnier: a starring role in one of our most popular detective dramas. Just imagine it: the next series of *Midsomer Murders* with the crack pairing of Barnier and Barnaby.

John Shewbridge
Weymouth, Dorset

SIR - Instead of using all those expensive resources and high-stakes political gamesmanship, we should just have played a game of rock, paper and scissors with the EU negotiators. Best of three gets to decide the exit rules.

Douglas Clerk
Stanley, Perthshire

SIR - Is there any correlation between the first pictures of a black hole and the present situation with the Brexit negotiations?

One of the lead astrophysicists described it as "looking into the face of hell".

David Wiltshire
Bedford

SIR - The European Council president Donald Tusk is right when he says there is a "special place in hell" for Brexiteers. It's called Brussels.

Michael Franklin
Tring, Hertfordshire

Bordering on the impossible

SIR - A 21st-century border with the EU giving virtually frictionless trade is eminently feasible. I propose it is called the "Unions Northern Ireland Co-operation On Road Networks" (Unicorn).

Martin Lewis
Haverfordwest, Pembrokeshire

SIR - Billy Connolly once explained that most Mexican fast food involves ingredients wrapped in the same doughy covering, which is simply folded in different ways.

I was reminded of this when reading about possible solutions to the issue of the post-Brexit Irish border.

Mick Andrews
Doncaster, South Yorkshire

SIR - Today, having woken in an expeditious frame of mind, I hauled myself out of bed and, in good faith, took the essential first step in beginning to apply my best endeavours to conclude, in due time, an ambitious framework agreement with myself to facilitate my future relationships on the allotment. I am seeing it as a sun-blessed, single customs territory where the perfectly formed vegetables, fruits and flowers are all good friends and partners, with the birds twittering cheerfully overhead and the insects and worms joyously doing insect and worm stuff. I recognise this won't happen overnight, and will require an extensive transition period. I have already put in place a backstop to avoid a hard border between the parsnips and carrots. Of course, freedom of movement is a given in any rotation system, though I will want to keep tabs on any stock wanting to dominate.

Other issues I need to look at:

- I think I might have too many amphibians in my pond.
- There's a large rock outcrop at the southern corner. That's a big job for the future.

At the moment, I've no place for the Brussels sprouts.

Phil Hulme
Manchester

The long goodbye

SIR – I am considering writing a book on the Brexit process: "From Here to Indefinitely".

Stephen Lawrence
Malvern Link, Worcestershire

SIR – Boris Johnson ends his article on the Brexit stalemate by quoting Exodus: "Let my people go". Does he mean that we will have to wander in the wilderness for 40 years before we reach the promised land?

James Nicholson
Southampton

SIR - The way the process is going, I think waiting for separation from the EU will be faster by continental drift than by legislation.

Steve Cattell
Grantham, Lincolnshire

SIR - In my efforts to keep up with the wall-to-wall coverage of Brexit, my dog has had to forgo some of her usual walks. In common with the rest of us, she cannot understand what is going on. So yesterday I felt obliged to let her have half an hour of *Dogs Behaving Badly*. She was as fascinated with that as I am with the Brexit debate - and for much the same reasons.

David Crawford
Llandudno, Conwy

The day peace was declared

SIR - Delighted to see the headline "Peace Treaty to be ready on 29 March". Unfortunately, it referred to the First World War.

Phil Cutcher
Malmesbury, Wiltshire

SIR - The clocks go back this weekend. I'm setting mine back to 1940 when our Prime Minister displayed leadership - sadly a very distant memory.

David Baron
Chichester, West Sussex

SIR - A bus whizzed past me recently with a poster declaring "Dumbo taking off on 29 March".

Is there a hidden Brexit message from the world of Disney here?

Philip Hirst
Ashton-under-Lyne, Lancashire

SIR - I recently bought a dress from a well-known middle-class catalogue company. It was made up of pieces of the Union flag, and I looked forward to wearing it on 29 March. Afterwards I intended to be buried in it or let it be passed on through my descendants as the "Brexit dress".

I now think that Brexit will be buried long before I am.

Dawn Latham
Reynoldston, Swansea

SIR - I bought a pack of fireworks to ignite when we left the EU on 29 March. On that non-event I resolved to launch one at 11pm on each set date we fail to leave, to give vent to my frustration.

There were only eight in the pack and I am now concerned I will not have enough.

Frances Williams
Swindon, Wiltshire

Fools' errand

SIR - I was saddened to read of the demise of Demo Cracy in your death notices on 1 April. I gather that her close friend, Parlia Ment, is also in bad shape. I wish her a speedy and complete recovery.

Jo-Ann Rogers
Stoke-on-Trent, Staffordshire

SIR - I hope the Withdrawal Agreement is now dead. It would be more accurately described as "coitus non-interruptus" as it's not actually a withdrawal from the European Commission's regulations, will cost us somewhere north of £39 billion and leave us holding a bouncing baby backstop that we're stuck with until it grows up, leaves school and gets a job.

Richard Elsy
Carlisle, Cumbria

SIR - If we are requested to vote in the next round of European elections I will vote with my feet, leaving a size 11 shoe print on the voting slip.

Douglas Clerk
Stanley, Perthshire

SIR - During the 2010 World Cup, an octopus named Paul had considerable success in predicting the outcome of matches. I wonder if a similarly prescient cephalopod could be found to guide the confused come the European elections on 23 May.

Dominic Weston Smith
Faringdon, Oxfordshire

Bumped in the night

SIR - The EU has postponed our leaving date to 31 October - are they planning a trick or treat?

Maria Daly
Loughborough, Leicestershire

SIR - Presumably the October deadline was chosen so that our senior civil servants and politicians could enjoy "the season", followed by a Mediterranean August holiday without interruption. Don't expect any progress until at least late September.

Alan Paine
Teignmouth, Devon

SIR - Nigel Farage has had a milkshake thrown over him during a walkabout in Newcastle.

In the 1970 general election campaign Harold Wilson was hit by eggs two days running, provoking the observation from Edward Heath that "This was a secret meeting on a secret tour which nobody is supposed to know about. It means that men - and perhaps women - are walking the streets with eggs in their pockets, just on the off-chance."

Are people now going around with milkshakes on the off-chance of seeing Mr Farage?

Christopher Horne
Rickmansworth, Hertfordshire

SIR - My initial thought on learning that a banana and salted caramel milkshake was thrown at Nigel Farage was

"How delicious, what a waste." I hope he licked his suit.

Dini Thorne
Smannell, Hampshire

A welcome departure

SIR – Is there any chance you might publish this letter? It's not about Brexit. It's not about anything else either, but it's NOT about Brexit.

J.L. Daniels
Liverpool

SIR – The best (and possibly only) good thing about the Brexit debate is that I can ignore the first eight pages of each day's newspaper.

Fred Wilson
Newcastle upon Tyne

SIR – Looking forward to all the unpublished letters on Brexit in next year's edition. Probably a volume on its own.

Ken Smart
Merriott, Somerset

SIR – Because of the wintry conditions, my copy of *The Daily Telegraph* was not delivered yesterday. To my astonishment, when normal service was resumed today, I found not a single reference to Brexit on your front page.

Could someone please tell me how it all ended?

J.F. Bailey
Henley-on-Thames, Oxfordshire

SIR - The only good feature I can see in the present situation is that everyone, just everyone, is suddenly interested in politics. At last.

Brian Foster
Shrivenham, Oxfordshire

Today's Luddites

SIR - I note that the three anti-fracking activists freed following their protest at Little Plumpton in Lancashire are from Sheffield, London and Devon. So much for local protest. This rent-a-mob rabble will only be satisfied when we have returned to a pre-industrial state, huddled outside caves and trying to figure out how to make something called a wheel out of a large piece of wood.

David S. Ainsworth
Manchester

Attack of the drones

SIR - A suitable punishment for any reckless drone operator who disrupts air traffic would be to condemn him/her to fly Ryanair for evermore.

Geoffrey Grimwood
Colwyn Bay, Conwy

SIR - I know plenty of guns that would enjoy a day popping drones over Gatwick.

Michael Heaton
Warminster, Wiltshire

SIR - I understand that the police are being given new powers to shoot down nuisance drones.

Is there any possibility that these powers could be extended to include wind chimes?

Anthony Baker
Poole, Dorset

Protesters are green as grass

SIR - The protest group Extinction Rebellion must be a collection of anarchists rather than environmentalists. Why would they make the London Underground a target? It's difficult to find a more efficient form of transport than an electric underground railway in a city.

Mark Robbins
Bruton, Somerset

SIR - A 17-year-old student protesting against climate change on a school day was quoted as saying: "Us leaving school means we show we value the climate the same as we value our education." So not a lot, then.

Clare Byam-Cook
London SW15

SIR - I understand there is a possibility that Greta Thunberg, the 16-year-old environmental champion from Sweden, will be invited to attend the UN climate summit in New York in September, and that she plans to get there by container ship. There is no need for her to use this polluting form of transport; if she set out now she could get there in good time by walking across the water.

Hugo Summerson
London SW20

SIR - As a woman slightly younger than Dame Emma Thompson, I last wore dungarees in the late Seventies. I am most intrigued as to where Dame Emma bought hers seemingly so readily for a protest, and can only conclude that she has borrowed them from the set of *Mamma Mia!*

Gilly Walker
Codford, Wiltshire

SIR - If the "climate activists" are sincere in their desire to reduce carbon dioxide emissions, perhaps they could do everyone a favour: stop breathing.

Amanda Stobbs
Shincliffe, County Durham

Novichok tactics

SIR - The Russian Novichok attackers showed fantastic incompetence in the actual assassination attempt, but genuine talent in managing to get from London to Salisbury on the Sunday train service.

Mick Ferrie
Mawnan Smith, Cornwall

SIR - I was delighted to read about our Russian visitors to Salisbury.

Perhaps the government could stretch to an all-expenses return trip for the same two individuals at their convenience. I suggest that the Old Bailey, Thames House, or the Royal Courts of Justice in London would appeal to them.

Ray Winstanley
Sheffield

SIR - Some years ago we bought a clock radio which is supposed to be satellite-linked, so that it always displays the correct time. Unfortunately, it's about 20 minutes fast.

Please could someone send me President Putin's number, so I can ask him to come round and take a look?

Alistair Halpern
London NW11

Old enough for Isil

SIR - I wonder how many of those advocating that "Isil bride" Shamima Begum was just a naïve and impressionable 15-year old when she was indoctrinated into joining and supporting the Islamic State of Iraq and the Levant also believe that 16-year-olds are mature, experienced and rational enough to be given the vote in elections.

Angus Long
Newcastle upon Tyne

SIR - I can't possibly comment on the fact that Shamima Begum considers that her British citizenship being revoked is "unjust".

I'm too busy choking on my lunch.

Louise Broughton
Bowness-on-Windermere, Cumbria

SIR - Jeremy Corbyn's call to allow Shamima Begum back into this country reminds me of an old clerical joke.

The last but one person to encounter the badly injured soul before the Good Samaritan came along was a social worker. They saw how terrible his wounds were, said "Gosh, the person who did this really needs some help", and left.

Keith Punshon
Thirsk, North Yorkshire

SIR - The only logical argument which I have seen to help decide what to do with the Begum girl is that, as with plastics, we should deal with our own rubbish.

Adair Anderson
Ravensheugh, Selkirk

Fire and fury

SIR - No matter what we think of US president Donald Trump and his forthcoming state visit, he has been elected after a democratic process. Perhaps Jeremy Corbyn and his ilk should save their ire for dictators who flout human rights, persecute their people and muzzle the media.

Kate Graeme-Cook
Brixham, Devon

SIR - I hope Jeremy Corbyn changes his socks daily. He seems to have his foot in his mouth almost every day.

Chris Platford
Malmesbury, Wiltshire

SIR - What a shame that - going by his attire to June's banquet with the Queen - Donald Trump's tailor doesn't know where a white waistcoat should end.

David Pound
Daventry, Northamptonshire

SIR - Here, we were all relieved that Michael Gove did not turn up in jogging kit.

Graham Fish
Hertford

We shall not see their like again

SIR - Let us hope that something similar to Operation Overlord never again needs to be organised.

The institutionalised leaking of government information, combined with the toxic environment of social media, would ensure that secrecy would be impossible to achieve.

Christopher Pratt
Dorking, Surrey

SIR - My father was the Squadron Clerk (Quartermaster Sergeant) for a fighter squadron supporting the British

Liberation Army and was in France not long after D-Day. I asked him what he had to obtain for the squadron and he said it was everything from bombs to bullets, tins of beans and bully beef to blankets and toilet paper. However, the bit that impressed me most as a boy was that he had managed to "liberate" a copy of *Mein Kampf* signed by a German officer.

Ted Shorter
Tonbridge, Kent

No fighting chance

SIR - You report on the performance of the firm Capita, with reference to the Armed Forces recruitment system.

The regard with which the company is held by many in the services is evidenced by the insertion of a strategically placed 'R' in its name.

Colin Cummings
Yelvertoft, Northamptonshire

SIR - Join the Army - your country needs you - but don't kill anybody or you may be charged with murder. And we wonder why recruitment is so difficult.

David Hughes
Camberley, Surrey

SIR - In 1942, at the age of 17, I went to the nearest Army's Home Guard HQ to be met by a sergeant who bellowed: "What do you want?"

"To join," I replied. "Piss off," he advised. So I went and joined the RAF, where I served for four years and eight months as a navigator/bomb aimer.

Upon relating this story many years later to a retired Army colonel, he said: "The Army got it right, then."

Duncan Bradbury
Bristol

SIR - The report on a successful year of trials for the aircraft carrier HMS Queen Elizabeth mentioned 202 take-offs and 187 landings for the F35 fighter jet. In my time in the RAF, we counted it a successful year if the number of take-offs and landings was more or less the same.

Nick Timms
Newark

SIR - The RAF is installing super-powered ejector seats to cater for 18-stone pilots. Good for them. However, will 10-stone pilots find themselves in orbit?

Brian Inns
Melksham, Wiltshire

Home guard

SIR - Reports that half of all burglaries take place when the owners are at home should do marvels for the sale of baseball bats.

Derek Long
Sheffield

SIR - I am concerned about the Home Secretary's directive that short sentences must be banned: must I now compose a few extra phrases or a subordinate clause or two to make my sentences of the appropriate length?

Jeremy Douglas-Jones
Swansea

SIR - It is so long since I saw a policeman on foot that I have started to watch reruns of *The Bill* to remind myself what they look like.

Chris Burdon
Rushmere St Andrew, Suffolk

Diagnosis: murder

SIR - The Home Secretary Sajid Javid says we must treat violence as a disease. "Sorry your Honour, I know I stabbed him but it's not my fault, I've got the violence disease."

Sandy Pratt
Pulborough, West Sussex

SIR - When I was a medical student my course failed to include instruction on the disease "violent crime". However, I did learn about it when I served on the local magistrates' bench for 26 years. The deterrent effect of a prison sentence goes some way towards preventing the disease.

Dr Dick Soper
Bury St Edmunds, Suffolk

SIR - I am glad to see that there are no longer going to be bars to prison cells, as my long-term aim is to end up in one of their rooms.

The healthcare is apparently excellent, the diet reasonable, the room and facilities adequate and the cost to one's family significantly less than paying for care in a home. An added bonus is that there is no waiting list.

John Wilson
Yeovil, Somerset

SIR - Prisons sensibly encourage inmates to take part in and improve their skills at various sports - but there is apparently a move, for good reasons, to ban any coaching of boxing and similar combat sports.

Surely it would be far more important to discourage any skills in pole vaulting and cross-country running.

David Whitaker
Alton, Hampshire

Full disclosure

SIR - Rather than using costly non-disclosure agreements and cowering under judicial skirts, prominent figures would do well to develop thick skins, adopt the noble example of the Duke of Wellington and say: "Publish and be damned." It did the Iron Duke no harm; he later served twice as Prime Minister.

John Bromley-Davenport QC
Malpas, Cheshire

SIR - Allison Pearson likens the beleaguered Topshop operator Sir Philip Green to an elephant seal wearing a wig. Normally I am a big fan of Allison's and, to be fair, she makes valid points in her otherwise excellent article - but who would want to be compared in looks, if nothing else, to Sir Philip?

Elephant seals cannot pay legal experts to speak up for them, nor silence any critics they may have.

David Porter
Barnet, Hertfordshire

No offence

SIR - Sajid Javid wants to classify ageism as a hate crime and declares his commitment to "stamping this sickening behaviour out". He needs to be careful that this statement is not construed as an incitement to commit an act of violence.

Gordon Garment
Chipping, Lancashire

SIR - Should ageism and misogyny become hate crimes, straight white middle-aged men would therefore become the only unprotected minority in the country.

Surely the time has come to start a campaign group to end this blatant discrimination against us. In the meantime, brothers, do not leave home without a dress and avoid pubs on pension day; it's dangerous out there.

Peter Lally
Broseley, Shropshire

SIR - I can no longer call the clerical collar a dog collar for fear of upsetting either my dog or my local vicar or both.

David Feilden
Solihull, West Midlands

SIR - The modern art of taking offence is rapidly being eclipsed by the political skill of taking offence vicariously.

The casualties are British gentle humour and the rainbow colours of the English language.

David Palmer
Jedburgh, Roxburghshire

Is it just me...?

SIR - Today I purchased a new diary. A quote at the bottom of one of the pages reads: "The world is so dreadfully managed, one hardly knows to whom to complain."

This, I think, nicely sums up my general mood.

Marguerite Beard-Gould
Walmer, Kent

SIR - Over the years I have attempted to engage my wife in discussion about politics. Her clear and consistent response has always been that "politics is b------s". I am beginning to think she may be on to something.

Ian Thompson
Ingst, Gloucestershire

SIR - Can everyone calm down? I don't just mean Brexit. It's everything. The nation seems to have been on a neurotic downward spiral ever since the millennium bug, and it's doing my head in. Thank you.

Anthony Tanney
Wickham Bishops, Essex

SIR - As another tumultuous political week draws to a close, it sometimes seems the entire world is on the brink of fractious collapse.

My bus to town must exist in a parallel dimension. Like many buses all over the world, it is full of pleasant people (and often sunshine too), letting each other sit down and quietly doing their bit to hold their community together. I think we'll be all right for another week.

James Dixon
Stanningfield, Suffolk

SPORTING
GLORY AND
DISASTER

A good innings

SIR - Should Alastair Cook decide to become a personal trainer in his retirement, I'll sign up. Have Senior Railcard, will travel.

Sheelagh James
Lichfield, Staffordshire

SIR - Four years ago, I wrote to your paper to suggest that the two most depressing words in the English language were "cricket highlights". I should like to change my mind.

Ruth Corderoy
East Hagbourne, Oxfordshire

SIR - I have just returned from my annual medical check-up, where I was told that my blood pressure and heart rate were very high.

"You a cricket fan?" the nurse asked.

On nodding I was told that I was the fourth of the day — and it was only 09:15.

Dr George Richards
Chester

SIR - Who are the masterminds who schedule cricket matches in Sri Lanka in the monsoon season and at Worcester in April?

Rosemary Kingsdown
Past President, Kent County Cricket Club
Sittingbourne, Kent

On yer bike

SIR - While watching the male triathletes with their name and country emblazoned on their pert posteriors, I observed that, were my bottom in the race, I could add all my sponsors and a warm message: "Welcome to the European Championships and have a nice day."

My husband responded: "And on the other cheek?"

Nicola Vernon
Epsom, Surrey

SIR - It surprises me that the organisers of the cycle race through the magnificent county of Yorkshire have named it with the French infliction *de*. Surely, those grand folk of England's largest county should be proud of their wonderful dialect and name it "Tour o' Yorkshire" instead of nodding to France. By 'eck, what's t'country coming to?

David Barnett
Griston, Norfolk

Football's own goal

SIR - If I had received £15 million for doing a thoroughly bad job, I would now be happily relaxing in my Sandbanks mansion.

Clearly, José Mourinho is a better man than me. His management and contractual skills obviously make him the best person to solve our Brexit fiasco.

Bob Pawsey
Hungerford, Berkshire

SIR - I have been watching women's football.

Does anyone know why women who play this game seem unable to dive, feign injury or roll about screaming?

Philip Saunders
Bungay, Suffolk

SIR - I was a parent at a prep school rugby match when I heard: "Perkins, do you know it's wrong to argue with the referee?"

"Yes, Sir," came the answer.

"You know booing is not acceptable, and you mustn't stamp your feet or make rude signs?"

"Yes, Sir."

"Well, go and tell your mother!"

Lt Cdr Alan Pearce RN (retd)
Verwood, Dorset

An off-putting new look

SIR - Having spent a very enjoyable weekend watching the Ryder Cup, I have been left wondering if the trousers the European team were wearing have some form of crotch reinforcement. I don't think ordinary stitching could hold out against the on-green stretching, bending and thrusting that was evident after a match win.

James Logan
Portstewart, County Londonderry

SIR - There is a trend for snooker players to wear waistcoats long enough to cover their buttocks. Is this because they no longer possess waists?

Sandra Hancock
Exeter, Devon

They shall go to the ball

SIR - It must surely be time for England's rugby players to find an antidote to the fearsome New Zealand haka.

I suggest a short Morris dance performance.

This should allow England to score at least one try before NZ has time to recover.

Richard Poole
Colchester, Essex

SIR - Wouldn't it be lovely if Remainers could show as much graciousness in defeat as the New Zealand cricket team and Roger Federer, who were beaten by even narrower margins?

Sue Cooper
Upper Hartfield, East Sussex

SIR - While sitting in the waiting room of a clinic at our local hospital last Wednesday, I was alarmed to hear loud cries of anguish. I became increasingly anxious about my appointment – until I noticed the television screen in the corner tuned in to Wimbledon. Phew!

Pam McEntyre
Chester

Nation of champions

SIR – It is heartening to read that crazy golf is gaining in popularity. While enjoying a round with my family in Maldon, Essex recently I scored two consecutive holes in one. A young couple following us asked if I was a professional.

John Pritchard
Ingatestone, Essex

SIR – Some years ago my husband and I travelled by train from Oxford to Paddington and spent a very pleasant hour doing a crossword, assisted by our seatmates, Sir Roger and Lady Bannister. I didn't realise who the gentleman was until we got off at Paddington and my husband said: "I think that's Roger Bannister." I couldn't let the opportunity pass, got back on the train and said, "Excuse me – my husband thinks you're Sir Roger Bannister." The response was: "I think I am too!"

Susan Fleck
Cheltenham, Gloucestershire

SIR – Long live the ladies of Liverpool at the Grand National meeting. Those who sneer at them deserve to be up before the stewards for excessive use of the whip. With their determination to have fun whatever the weather, they are an essential addition to the festive spirit of the occasion – good luck to them.

Lucinda Roberts
Lapford, Devon

THAT'S
ENTERTAINMENT

Creature features

SIR - In the light of recent demands that characters in films, television and theatre be played by actors of the same race, gender, sexual orientation and/or disability, I await the inevitable protests from the Klingon, Orc and Dalek "communities" at always being portrayed by human beings in make-up, suits and prosthetics.

Andrew Williamson
Gateshead, Tyne and Wear

SIR - Although I find the meerkats in the television ads amusing, I have often wondered why they have Russian names and accents when the species' natural habitat is southern Africa. One theory is that they are refugees from a famine in the Kalahari - but if so, why didn't they claim asylum in the first safe country they reached?

Michael Wood-Wilson
Leigh-on-Sea, Essex

Drama queens

SIR - Julie Burchill describes the Oscars as "a love-in for smug, posturing hypocrites".
   Well, we've also got one of those - it's called Parliament.

Roger Chappell
Coventry, Warwickshire

SIR - Congratulations to Olivia Colman upon her award of a BAFTA for her role as Queen Anne, but is she really on her way to becoming a national treasure? I hope not. I cannot imagine Julie Andrews, Celia Johnson, Vivien Leigh or Olivia de Havilland including in an acceptance speech the line: "We are going to get so p----- later."

Shaun Whyte
Alnmouth, Northumberland

SIR - My local multiplex cinema claims to be showing "Mary Queen of Scotts". Is this a film about the inventor of porridge oats?

John Bowden
Chellaston, Derbyshire

SIR - To play the next James Bond I nominate Jodie Comer, a perfect mix of devilishness and cruelty as Villanelle in *Killing Eve*. Bond is, after all, a psychopath.

Peter Gamble
Cirencester, Gloucestershire

SIR - What is this nonsense about the lead role in *Doctor Who* being given to a woman for the first time? I can assure you that when Katy Manning played companion Jo Grant hers was the central character.

J.G. Riseley
Harrogate, North Yorkshire

Battle weary

SIR - How is it possible that so many viewers (globally) can be deliriously excited by *Game of Thrones*?

To see what the fuss is about I watched part of the "battle" episode. All we got were forlorn medieval types in dull garb swinging at each other for hours on end. Bring on a few wheezing dragons and the Night King, who was about as frightening as an old sock wearing a nightie, and there we have it.

Keith Day
Portstewart, County Londonderry

Young and promising

SIR – Watching *Gogglesprogs* at present. Maybe they should form a new government.

John Stevenson
Maidenhead, Berkshire

Scheduling difficulties

SIR – We have just enjoyed what I call my Hour of Humiliation on Monday evening television: *Only Connect* followed by *University Challenge*.

Jessica Findlay
Cullen, Banffshire

SIR – I am pleased to note that Channel 4 is showing *100 Vaginas*. This is immediately followed in the TV listings by *Naked Attraction*. Good programming.

Robbie Wolfson
Knutsford, Cheshire

SIR – Having spent a fortune creating their latest *Luther* TV drama series, perhaps the BBC could tell us why they filmed it in the dark. We could have watched it on radio at a fraction of the cost.

Brian Christley
Abergele, Conwy

The soap bubble's burst

SIR - Given the huge rise in costs for refurbishing the set of *Eastenders*, perhaps it is time for the BBC to take the advice proffered by at least one of the characters in most episodes: "Leave it love, it ain't worth it!"

Ruth Corderoy
East Hagbourne, Oxfordshire

SIR - I would like to live long enough to see the final episode of the never-ending *Coronation Street*.

Hyder Ali Pirwany
Okehampton, Devon

SIR - Your article on *The Archers* reminded me of my intense disappointment as a seven-year-old when the long-awaited new programme proved not to be about Robin Hood.

Ian Metcalfe
Perth

SIR - I think *The Archers* reflects the current state of the country. When you think things can't get worse, they do.

Gabrielle Williams
Beaumaris, Anglesey

Costume drama

SIR - There seems to be a competition on the BBC's breakfast news as to who can wear the brightest blouses. By the time my eyes have been assaulted with garish colours and my ears subjected to the same old depressing stories, I want to give up on life and go back to bed.

Barbara Read
Sherborne, Dorset

SIR - It is high time for the BBC to require its news presenters to wear the burka.

The same garment, worn daily, would save a considerable amount on dress allowance. There would be no need for make-up either.

Marcus Bradley
Worcester

SIR - With the advent of equality and a reduction in salaries it has become noticeable over the past few months that the male news staff on the BBC appear unable to afford the luxury of neckties.

In order to help the Corporation maintain standards, I appeal to wearers who might otherwise send their old ties to landfill to donate to those in need.

David Belcher
Thatcham, Berkshire

Brought into question

SIR - *The Jeremy Kyle Show* - a confrontational TV programme, described by a judge as a bear-pit, in which accusations are hurled back and forth and participants are shouted down with a presenter forced to try and maintain a semblance of order - has been cancelled by ITV.

Can we now expect the BBC to withdraw Prime Minister's Questions?

John Hellings
Emsworth, Hampshire

SIR - Fiona Bruce's first *Question Time* - proof everything in this nation isn't doomed to get worse.

Not so much a breath of fresh air as a long overdue gale force wind of change for the better.

Mark Boyle
Johnstone, Renfrewshire

SIR - I am convinced that Fiona Bruce gets Theresa May's cast-off short and stupid jackets.

Allan J. Eyre
Middlesbrough, North Yorkshire

Break up the BBC

SIR - If the average age of BBC One viewers is over 61, why does the broadcaster not do as ITV does and have a lavatory stop every 15 minutes?

My wife and I both in our mid-eighties - would appreciate this.

Derrick G. Smith
Bexhill-on-Sea, East Sussex

SIR – The BBC has polled 190,000 people and 52 per cent are in favour of abolishing free TV licences for the over-75s. I trust that this will result in outraged retainers pushing for a delay in the implementation and a second referendum.

Janet Gould
Huntingdon, Cambridgeshire

SIR – We have been subjected to bullying letters from TV Licensing, even though we have been without a television for over 30 years.

Twenty years ago we did actually have a visit from an enforcement officer. I took the man around the house, and when we reached the last room said: "Would you like to come in the bedroom?"

He disappeared rather quickly!

June Small
Taunton, Somerset

SIR – I sent my son off to university with a black-and-white television set. He coped with the indignity but his flatmates found watching the snooker frustrating.

David Shaw
Codford, Wiltshire

Nothing to report

SIR – My New Year's resolution was to stop watching and listening to the BBC news. I feel more positive and cheerful about the future already and recommend this course of inaction to everyone.

Nigel Milliner
Truro, Cornwall

SIR – Just turned on to the BBC news channel. It showed a vehicle exiting on a motorway slip road with a very large orange sign for those going the other way, which said in large letters:

DANGER
WRONG WAY
TURN BACK

Is this for lost motorists or politicians?

Graham Hart
Leicester

SIR – The *Today* programme would not be the same without John Humphrys. It would be possible to hear what the interviewees have to say.

Kevin Heynes
Heath Charnock, Lancashire

SIR – It's me! I'm the one! The only British citizen who's not been invited onto Radio 4 to give my opinion. Does no one care what I think?

Roger Noons
Kingswinford, West Midlands

SIR - I do at least try to follow Brexit news by listening to Evan Davis on Radio 4, but often I need a diversion. I turn to a CD of The Beach Boys, and listening to *Don't Worry Baby* cheers me up. Unfortunately it is immediately followed by *God Only Knows*.

Pamela Farnworth
Gargrave, North Yorkshire

SIR - The (not always accurate) television captions on the midday BBC news spoke of the "free bra" of Brexit. This was, to me, surprising and uplifting news among the general gloom.

Chris Lee
Callington, Cornwall

SIR - Congratulations to the BBC for finding those ridiculous stools for the Tory leadership debate. It certainly succeeded in making all the candidates look absurd.

Gabriella Marlesford
Woodbridge, Suffolk

SIR - It seems a tacky summer reality show is once again enthralling millions.

It comprises preening narcissists, mostly talking rubbish, desperately trying to make themselves popular, pursuing "bedfellows".

The contest is likely to be won by a blond.

But enough of the Conservative leadership contest. Meanwhile, *Love Island* continues nightly on ITV2.

David Stanley
London SW6

Euro stars in their eyes

SIR – I cannot claim to be a fan of the Eurovision Song Contest, and can only recall "Puppet on a String" sung by shoeless Sandie Shaw some time ago.

However, I really must stand up for this year's British entry, and wish him the very best fortune, as sharing his name has bought me some notoriety in the local bridge club.

Michael Rice
Chichester, West Sussex

SIR – Madonna said at Eurovision that music brings people together. So, Andrew Lloyd Webber, what are you waiting for? The time has come for *Brexit: The Musical*.

Ken Page
Hexham, Northumberland

Duty calls

SIR – I am so glad I haven't watched *Line of Duty*. I feel I saved many hours of my life. But then again I did watch *Fleabag*, so no net gain.

Mark Solon
London E1

SIR – I have never watched *Line of Duty*, so have no idea what it is about. However, it would seem from recent comments that faithful viewers are equally baffled.

Jill Champion
Braintree, Essex

SIR - "Ice Age Mammoth bones found on motorway site", runs your headline. A case for the *Unforgotten* team?

Hugh Gill
St Lawrence, Jersey

Heaven knows we're Misérable now

SIR - In over 50 years of theatre going I've only ever walked out once and that was after the first act of *Les Mis*. A more aptly named show I've never encountered.

Alan Hewer
Seaford, East Sussex

SIR - I am fond of costume dramas. My favourite is *Robocop*.

Richard Veys
Rugby, Warwickshire

HOME
THOUGHTS ON
ABROAD

Vive la revolution

SIR – The thugs who killed a family of swans in protest against the monarchy might like to go and live in a republic. France is nearby and there is a tradition there of violent protests, so they should feel at home.

Unfortunately, they'd have to put up with Emmanuel Macron (not a patch on the Queen) and learn to sing the interminable *Marseillaise* (which even French people don't know all the words to).

Virginia Price Evans
Whitland, Carmarthenshire

SIR – The "yellow vest" protests in France have inspired me to suggest an addition to the English dictionary: *JillyJohn* n. Someone who participates in unfocused and anarchic demonstrations against the established order (see Corbynite).

Clive Smith
Tarporley, Cheshire

SIR – The rural "yellow vests" say they are heading for a bigger revolution than in 1789. As a recently retired magician, I have a redundant guillotine for sale.

Ian Marriott
Romsey, Hampshire

SIR – At my local supermarket I noticed staff wearing yellow jackets with the slogan "Happy to help" on the back. Surely, if we take to the streets, this is what we should wear. It would be the British way of doing things.

Michael Johnston
Tollesbury, Essex

Love for Our Lady of Paris

SIR - A lasting memory of my first visit to Notre-Dame cathedral in 1952 is of being offered dirty postcards immediately outside the door of the north tower. Happily the memory of the fabulous west rose window surmounts the pornographer.

Jeremy Watson
Marnhull, Dorset

SIR - Windsor, Glasgow School of Art, York Minster and Notre-Dame were all undergoing restoration when fire broke out. Perhaps we should be taking pre-emptive precautions at Westminster, as I cannot imagine anyone putting in £100 million to save our current politicians' gaff.

Charles Shaw
Warrington, Cheshire

Entente trop cordiale

SIR - I was alarmed by the photograph of the embrace between Mrs May and Monsieur Macron in Paris. I feel she is too young for him.

Paul Rumbold
Holcombe, Lancashire

SIR - A macron is a symbol on a letter to stress and elongate a vowel sound.

My response to Emmanuel Macron's machinations is a stress of a consonant: *aghhhhhhhhhhhh*.

John Bergin
Oxton, Wirral

SIR - President Macron is unfortunately becoming more and more similar to his near namesake, the French confectionery the macaron. Much more nauseating than one originally anticipated.

Kim Dace
Brenchley, Kent

SIR - Boris Johnson's idea of having a Channel bridge to France could be conceived as forward-thinking, green and innovative, especially if it is a cycle path. Since the Green Party wants to restrict individuals to a single flight per annum, we could cycle back from our holidays in Europe. All suggestions for saddle soreness will be gratefully received.

Andy Hussey
Burnham-on-Crouch, Essex

Out and proud

SIR - Strolling past the famed Cockring Disco in Amsterdam in the mid-Eighties, my partner and I were approached by a very friendly leather-clad local gentleman and invited to attend later that evening. On being advised that it was "kit off" after nine o'clock, we expressed our reservations. We were informed that this was a common reaction among British visitors and told that a special dispensation existed for the British, namely "pants on".

Might this be the earliest example of a UK EU opt-out?

Joe Horton
Aylesbury, Buckinghamshire

Barmy EU Army

SIR - One can imagine a European Armed Forces. A flight of executive jets but no airforce, dozens of expensive staff cars but no tanks, a fleet of executive yachts but no navy and of course dozens of staff officers but no combatants.

The only threat it would pose to Russia's President Putin is that he might die laughing.

Andrew Cranshaw
Cranbrook, Kent

SIR - There has been some concern for Germany's chancellor Angela Merkel, as she was seen shaking and trembling during the playing of the German national anthem.

That's usually the effect it has on the French and Belgians.

John Kennedy
Hornchurch, Essex

Reach for the stars

SIR - I was delighted to hear the Israelis have successfully launched their space programme, but I wonder if they realise that they are now one step closer to qualifying for a payment from Britain's overseas aid budget.

If they can now prove that they have a pop group that can tick the diversity box, they will be almost home and dry.

Simon Tuck
Seer Green, Buckinghamshire

Twitterer-in-chief

SIR – With all these tweets and twitters coming out of Washington, I wonder what sort of birdbrain is in charge.

John M. Tennant
Woolhampton, Berkshire

SIR – Despite many of my friends exhorting me to join the regiment of people writing books about Donald Trump, I will not do so.

I am instead writing a book to be entitled "The sTRUMPets", but so far all I have managed is the title.

V.S. Payne
Nottingham

SIR – Following a recent holiday passed mainly in the company of Americans, one begins to realise why Donald Trump was elected.

Michael J. Collins
Cowbeech, East Sussex

De-fence is the best form of attack

SIR – President Trump is about 700 years late in his call
for the wall to keep out immigrants. The Native Americans
should have had one to stop the religious bigots invading
in the name of crackpot religious ideas and rapacious
invaders, who in rapid time destroyed the people and
animals in two vast continents.

Bill Jolly
Lancaster

SIR – "Give me your tired, your poor, Your huddled
masses yearning to breathe free, The wretched refuse of
your teeming shore." These are the words on the Statue
of Liberty. Since this doesn't seem to apply to those trying
to escape from appalling conditions in South and Central
America, can we expect to see the mothballing of the iconic
statue on President Trump's to-do list?

Paula Nicholson
Heathfield, East Sussex

The art of the deal

SIR – President Trump has walked away from a long-
awaited, high-stakes deal with North Korean leader Kim
Jong-un, citing "no deal is better than a bad deal".
   Theresa May: watch and learn.

Caroline Bullock
Reading, Berkshire

SIR - Mr Trump has said that he "knows when to walk". Would it be possible for someone to offer him a pirate's plank?

ECL, via email

SIR - Donald Trump and Kim Jong-un - the summit of the world's two weirdest hairdos.

Rosemary Marshall
New Malden, Surrey

Lost in translation

SIR - Some years ago I received a picture postcard from a friend who was on holiday abroad. The postcard was festooned with stamps all around the edges and down the centre, leaving only space for the address and the message. It read: "When buying stamps at a French post office, it is important to know the difference between *cinq* and *cinquante*."

Chris Bocock
Quorn, Leicestershire

SIR - About ten years ago I went to China, and had promised to send a postcard to the staff of my local building society. This I duly did from Xian, home of the terracotta warriors. I headed it *XIAN*.

On my return, I asked the staff whether they had received it.

"No," came the reply. "Only one headed 'Love Ian'."

M.I. Hesselberg
Liverpool

SIR - Thanks to my South American Spanish phrasebook of 1996, I am able to ask any passing Spaniard: "Is this a hallucinogenic cactus?"

Sue Abel
Alderney, Guernsey

That undiscovered country

SIR - I am always intrigued by the planning thoughts behind the design of the layout at Dublin airport.

On the final approach to the airport, the last thing you see before landing is a neat cemetery - and for the return flight, one of the last road signs before Terminal 2 is for the mortuary.

Lovat Timbrell
Brighton, East Sussex

SIR - In the old days when passengers could occasionally sit in the flight-deck jumpseat, I was delighted to reach my one millionth air mile flying into JFK New York. Due to heavy traffic, the landing had to be aborted - so I added an extra 30-odd miles towards my next million as we went around.

I was also given a signed flightplan and a bottle of champagne, though the latter had to be disguised under a napkin as I exited the cockpit so as not to alarm the other passengers.

Jeremy Burton
Wokingham, Berkshire

Kilroy was here

SIR - Where is Kilroy?

Thirty or forty years ago it was difficult to visit places without coming across evidence that Kilroy had been there first. He was widely travelled and left his simple message all over the world. Often, in moments of loneliness, it seemed that he was the only "friend" one had.

But now it seems that Kilroy is no longer on the move, his travels curtailed - perhaps by illness, lack of finance, detention without trial or even death itself, although scrutiny of the obituary columns has failed to corroborate this.

Peter Ferry
Moulsford, Oxfordshire

TRAVEL IN
BRITAIN

Pot luck

SIR – Given the Chancellor's bumper £14.9 billion budget surplus, for the sake of my teeth fillings, would it not be possible to ask for a teeny weeny proportion of this amount to be spent on repairing potholes?

Robert Wilson
Barby, Northamptonshire

SIR – Your headline tells us that "potholes kill more in India than acts of terror".

It's the same here in Devon.

Adrian LLoyd-Edwards
Dartmouth, Devon

A heavy toll

SIR – Removing the Severn tolls has now made it free for the English to come to Wales to steal our Welsh daughters.

Leslie Watson
Swansea

Going steady

SIR – I notice the doctor in *Call the Midwife* has changed his car. The previous one brought back fond memories of when my husband courted me in his 1956 MG Magnette. This leaked oil on my parents' drive, prompting my mother to say, "Can't you go out with someone with a decent car?" It proved its worth by accomplishing the overland journey to Kabul, Afghanistan, in 1971.

Gay Reynolds
Little Chalfont, Buckinghamshire

SIR - Charles Moore highlights the dangers caused by elderly drivers. I had myself begun to wonder what had happened to the little old man in the flat cap peering through the steering wheel. Then I looked in my rear-view mirror and realised he had become me.

Simon Watson
Petworth, West Sussex

SIR - It is reported that drivers who pass a cycling test could get cheaper insurance.

I have found my Cycling Proficiency Certificate, awarded in 1962. Should I now use this to ask my car insurer for a discount?

Peter Calver
Knebworth, Hertfordshire

SIR - While at school in the Sixties, I passed my cycling proficiency test three times. I took it three years running to get out of geography lessons.

Anthony Liddicoat
Ongar, Essex

SIR - Yesterday in the City of Derby, I saw a cyclist stop at a red traffic light and wait patiently. I may never see it again but I will cherish the memory.

Terry Lloyd
Derby

On track for life

SIR - The introduction of a "millennial" railcard is one step forward in a zero-sum game. Once everyone qualifies for a railcard, the "concessionary" aspect disappears. There are already 37 categories of railcard on offer: one just needs a mid-life crisis card to complete the set.

Peter Harper
Salisbury, Wiltshire

SIR - How is it that whenever I am on a train, I am surrounded by people who do not carry handkerchiefs?

David Nunn
West Malling, Kent

SIR - Today my train has been cancelled because high winds risked blowing it off the track. Yesterday it was late because water on the rails was reducing the wheel traction and the speed at which it was able to pull away from the station.

   The Department of Lame Excuses has obviously been given some more money.

Paul Bendit
Arlington, East Sussex

If stones could talk

SIR - In recent weeks the electronic signboards upon joining the M3 from the M25 have informed me of delays at Stonehenge. They started it 5,000 years ago, and the last time I looked the roof still wasn't on.

Who's running that project? Theresa May?

Christopher Monniot
Crawley, West Sussex

SIR - I read Harry Mount's article about Stonehenge with
great interest, but it did nothing to cause me to alter my
personal view about its origins. My theory is that the stones
were being transported from one side of the country to the
other, when those bearing it lost interest in the project,
said "Sod it!", and dumped them on Salisbury Plain, where
they happened to be at the time.

Ross Bourne
Salisbury, Wiltshire

Just passing through

SIR - On one occasion when my wife and I were staying at
our favourite Lake District inn, the owner had gone into
the roof space above our room to get a piece of carpet when
his foot slipped off the rafters and came through the ceiling
just above our bed. At the end of the holiday, my wife wrote
in the visitors' book: "It was nice of Geoff to drop in, but
next time could he come through the door."

Chris King
Woking, Surrey

SIR - In his last book, Professor Stephen Hawking wrote
that time travel "can't be ruled out".
  If he is right, why are there no historical records of
medieval towns and villages being visited by futuristically

dressed Japanese tourists taking selfies with the locals outside their rudimentary dwellings?

Geoff Johnson
Gateshead, Tyne and Wear

SIR - Surely ghosts, or most of them, are simply time-travellers from a future when such things will be possible, passing through our era on their way to study an earlier period, and dressed accordingly.

Tim Topps
Oxford

Incompetent showers

SIR - My wife and I have been taking holidays in France since the late Seventies.

Such were the vagaries of the showers we came across in hotels that I decided they should meet three basic criteria: they should have directional stability, meaning that the water should be capable of being aimed at the user; the water temperature should be controllable, and the water should remain in the shower cubicle.

Our quest has continued for almost 40 years, and I can report that we have never found one that met all three criteria.

Ed Mackrill
Birchwood, Cheshire

SIR - A bath is a bath - but a shower is an adventure.

Patricia Wallis
Boston, Lincolnshire

SIR - Terse instructions seen on a Japanese trouser press in a Yorkshire hotel.

1. *Remove trouser*
2. *Insert trouser*
3. *Power on*
4. *Retire*
5. *Arise and enjoy trouser.*

Frank W. Mancktelow
Kemsing, Kent

Signs of the times

SIR - Driving on the M4 recently, I passed what was clearly a warning sign - in Welsh (though not being a Welsh speaker I did not understand it). About a mile later I caught up with the English version, informing me in the usual nannying fashion about "poor driving conditions".

Are Welsh-reading drivers so much more accident-prone than their English counterparts that they need to be warned first, or is there some pro-Welsh language bias at work here which favours the former group while the latter are expected to take their chances for a further mile?

Gary Spring
Wareham, Dorset

SIR - In the late Sixties I often passed in South Devon a road sign that read: "Do not shoot at this sign".

In 1972 it was replaced with a new one with the same legend, the old one having been ravaged by rifles and shotguns being fired at it. I never found a person who could tell me what it was there for.

Viv J. Seymour
Worthing, West Sussex

SIR - The village of Four Marks in Hampshire once had its roadside name board embellished overnight with the words: "Out of ten". They were very quickly scrubbed off.

Joanna Sharpe
Pitton, Wiltshire

SIR - With the name of Wool under threat from vegans, I only hope they do not hear about my village.

Brian Lawrence
Hamstreet, Kent

There once was a chap on the road...

SIR - Like the Duchess of Cornwall, I recite poems to myself in bed. I have hundreds if not thousands tucked away in my hippocampus. When driving I have an urge to conjure up limericks from the place names I see, but so far have failed with Llanfairpwllgwyngyllgogerychwyrndrobwllll-lantysiliogogogoch.

Dr Robert J. Leeming
Coventry, Warwickshire

ROYAL
RELATIONS

Prince of the people

SIR – The warmth generated by the Prince of Wales'
use of pidgin on a visit to West Africa reminded me of a
colleague who had to give some guidance to a group of
friendly African farmers on a sponsored visit to Britain.
The individual farmers came from several Commonwealth
countries.

It happened that the farmers were to meet the Queen
and were given a crash course on protocol. They were
advised that initiating a conversation with the enquiry "How
de body?" might not be appropriate. Who's to know, Her
Majesty might have enjoyed the exchange.

John S. Davidson
Ferndown, Dorset

SIR – Prince Charles has pledged that he will not be a
"meddling" monarch.

When one views the antics of one's government, one very
often longs for a meddling king (or queen).

Martin Smith
Brimpsfield, Gloucestershire

SIR – Your photographs of the Prince of Wales wearing
smart trousers and pristine white shirt with tie, whether
working on important papers in his garden or feeding his
chickens, made a delightful spread. As with Clive Dunn
in his role of Corporal Jones in *Dad's Army*, the Prince has
finally grown old enough to wear the clothes which he has
been sporting for the past 50 years.

William T. Nuttall
Rossendale, Lancashire

Thoroughly modern Meghan

SIR - I was surprised to note that the Duchess of Sussex chose to defy British convention and appear bare-shouldered when attending the Royal Gala Performance in London. I'm all for change, but not when it is totally unnecessary. Go unchecked and next time the good lady could appear in jeans and a T-shirt.

Roger Harris
Monmouth

On his grandmother's secret service

SIR - Does the news that the Duke of Cambridge has engaged in three weeks' "work experience" with the security services indicate that the film industry has finally settled on the person to succeed Daniel Craig as James Bond?

GA, via email

God save the Queen's consort

SIR - In view of the Duke of Edinburgh's miraculous escape following a car accident, it would seem that the divinity of the monarch remains in place.

Paul Cheater
Dorchester, Dorset

SIR — In his tweeted prayer to the Almighty, seeking blessings and happiness for Prince Philip following his accident, The Archbishop of York, John Sentamu, omits any mention of the other parties involved.

Let us hope that God is a *Telegraph* reader and is aware of the facts, that He might include them in his bounty too.

James L. Shearer
Edinburgh

SIR - The BBC reports that the Duke of Edinburgh will not be driving on public highways "going forward". Does this mean that in future he will be driving in reverse gear?

David White
Exeter, Devon

Ups and downs of the Grand Old Duke

SIR - I am becoming increasingly concerned about the Duke of York and his whereabouts. His continuous travel arrangements have not been gazetted in your Court Circular recently. Is he ill? Is he marooned abroad?

Greig Bannerman
Frant, East Sussex

#BabySussex

SIR - In the current spirit of abbreviating everything (Brexit, etc), to save time, in referring to the forthcoming royal baby, may I suggest "Preghan"?

Joe Greaves
Fleckney, Leicestershire

SIR - I would like to express my dismay at yet another royal child, since his arrival pushes me still further back in the line of succession.

Bob Hope said that when he realised that he would never become king, that's when he emigrated to the United States. I am beginning to empathise with him.

Dr E.S. Garbett
Sheffield

SIR - It is rumoured that the Most Reverend Michael Curry, the American cleric who officiated at Harry and Meghan's wedding, has sent them a 5,000-word telegram congratulating them on the new royal baby.

Peter Anderson
Kettering, Northamptonshire

SIR - I have some sympathy with Danny Baker, who has apparently been sacked for a rather tasteless tweet about chimpanzees and royal babies.

When I first met my daughter in the delivery room I was struck by her deep red hair. I told my wife that she looked like an orang-utan, which I considered to be a great compliment. My wife, unfortunately, did not see it as such.

Dr Charles Gallimore
Oakham, Rutland

As yet untitled

SIR - How can new parents need more time to think about names for their new arrival? If they haven't come up with a choice of names for the baby by the time it arrives, what have they been doing for the last nine months?

Mike Tugby
Warminster, Wiltshire

SIR – To anyone of my generation, the only famous Archie is Archie Andrews, the ventriloquist's dummy, who had his own radio series *Educating Archie* in the Fifties. He was also the first dummy to be made into a dummy when he was awarded a place in Madame Tussaud's.

I once interviewed Archie Andrews for a BBC radio programme I was making. It was a phone interview. His voice sounded very similar to that of his owner Peter Brough.

Jeremy Nicholas
Great Bardfield, Essex

SIR – We have a Scottish terrier of uncertain temperament called Archie. Now that a royal has been named for him, he thinks it is his right to sit on the best chair.

Freda Murray
Tewkesbury, Gloucestershire

USE AND ABUSE
OF LANGUAGE

A pronounced problem

SIR - It seems that fewer and fewer people are capable of pronouncing the letter "T" these days. With the start of the new year, many have wished me a "happy twennie ninedeen."
  I look forward to the "star of twennie twennie".

Richard Hodder
Four Elms, Kent

SIR - Exactly where is this Mount Killymanjaro to which BBC Comic Relief presenters have been referring?
  I think it must be in Wales.

Paul Blundell
Daventry, Northamptonshire

SIR - Is World Bee Day (20 May) a time for global posterior ablutions?

Alison Pascoe
Cheltenham, Gloucestershire

All very well

SIR - I see that Goldman Sachs has Laura Young as head of wellness. We now need to know if her assistant has the job title "head of slightly-less-wellness".

Peter Owen
Woolpit, Suffolk

SIR - I was touched many years ago when a shop assistant in a large department store came up to me and said: "Are you alright there?"

I had a slight cold, and I described my symptoms to the lady in question, thanking her for her concern. This morning, having been asked the same question for possibly the thousandth time, I'm getting a little self-conscious about this constant concern for my health. Do they know something I don't?

Andrew Sturmey
Selby, North Yorkshire

I must protest

SIR - I am less concerned by the Oxford Union's invitation to the far-right German politician Alice Weidel to speak than by the transmogrification of "platform" from a noun to a verb ("no-platforming") by supposedly well-educated students.

Philip Barry
Dover, Kent

SIR - People used to be called out when you needed help or an urgent repair, or when there was a strike. Now every interview seems to involve somebody being called out when they are merely being challenged. Time to call time on calling out.

Ian Huish
Banbury, Oxfordshire

In, out, shake it all about

SIR - Why is a "no deal" Brexit referred to as *crashing out*? I always thought that one crashes *into* things.

Steve Maton
Salisbury, Wiltshire

SIR - What's the alternative to *crashing out*? Frozen in? Gagged in? Plunged in? Chained in?

Ruth Wright
Leigh-on-Sea, Essex

SIR - Remainers can crash out if they want to; Brexiteers prefer to leave.

Judith Riches
Wellington Heath, Herefordshire

The People's cliché

SIR - First it was the perennial "People's Choice", the "People's Car", then, God help us, the "People's Princess" - quickly and currently followed by the "People's Vote".

One good reason for never voting Labour, especially under its current leadership, is that, quick as a flash, they will call everything "The People's" something or other and then make absolutely sure that the "people" never get so much as a sniff of it. We're not the right kind of people, you see.

Hugh Rogers
Ashby, North Lincolnshire

SIR - Listening to various news reports, can someone please clarify whether the government has agreed a deal on *Brexit* or *Bregzit*, and how the two options might differ?

Caroline Barr
Much Wenlock, Shropshire

SIR - Brexit has destroyed grammar. I keep hearing, "I don't want no deal."

Thinking of Mick Jagger, I suppose none of us will get no satisfaction.

R. Allan Reese
Dorchester

SIR - When we finally leave the EU, presumably we will need new terms to describe Remainers and Brexiteers. I suggest *Rejoiners* and *Rejoicers*, to describe the two factions that will then exist.

Stephen Kirby
Charing, Kent

SIR - The latest crop of Brexit arguments and discussions include some stock phrases that are beginning to get annoyingly repetitive.

The clock ticking down, kicking the can down the road and *chasing unicorns* are the main offenders.

Perhaps we could encourage the use of an all-encompassing phrase, such as "the unicorn kicking the clock down the road".

Ron Pulford
Tarporley, Cheshire

Absolute zero

SIR - Health Secretary Matt Hancock says the NHS will adopt a "zero tolerance" approach to violence against its staff. This is obviously laudable; however, for peace of mind, might the government kindly confirm what level of violence it believes should be tolerated against non-NHS workers, if above zero?

Simon Millar
Poole, Dorset

SIR - Need one be employed in the public sector, notably the NHS, to be an "unsung hero"? Are there any unsung heroes in, say, financial services?

Paul Rumbold
Holcombe, Lancashire

SIR - I am tired of reading or hearing that a terrorist was "inspired" by Isil. Surely inspiration is good. We are inspired by artists, architects, scientists, poets, authors and many other kinds of people. Terrorists are brainwashed or influenced by Isil.

Joan Freeland
Exeter, Devon

SIR - If the American vice-president Mike Pence is correct there is much cause for concern, for had the Islamic State caliphate been "decimated", as he has claimed, then 90 per cent would have remained intact and presented a serious threat.

Fortunately it is not so.

Jonathan Reeves
Bromley, Kent

SIR - How many Olympic swimming pools are there in a Royal Albert Hall?

David Oliver
Langley, Berkshire

Colour me confused

SIR - I would be very grateful if someone could explain to me the difference between being referred to as a *woman of colour* (good) and a *coloured woman* (bad - apparently).

Barry Westwood
New Malden, Surrey

SIR - Whether we like the term or not, everyone in the world is coloured. Currently I'm bordering on Middleton Pink.

Robert Warner
Ramsbury, Wiltshire

SIR - I like to think that I am "woke"; however, not after a heavy lunch or when I am asleep.

Peter Martinez
Chagford, Devon

Pardon your Scots

SIR - Did I really read in *The Daily Telegraph* of "jiggery-pokery"?

Where I come from, jiggery-pokery is allied to slap-and-tickle and rumpy-pumpy - except that in the season of

Robert Burns, we employ the thoroughly more wholesome Scots term "houghmagandie".

Gordon Casely
Crathes, Kincardineshire

SIR - I was amused to see that your article on "Free the Nipple" campaigners was co-written by James TITcomb. Ouch!

Amanda Malas
Hartley, Kent

No more jobs for the boys

SIR - Counting my cherry pits - tinker, tailor, soldier, sailor, etc - I was struck that all the choices are male. In this day and age should there not be a female list, or perhaps one that is non-gender specific?

Lindsay Marsh
Farnham, Surrey

SIR - Do we now have to say "As the actor said to the bishop"?

G. Plowden
London W2

SIR - I am not sure the implications of gender-neutral shipping have been fully thought through. I'll shave my belly with a rusty razor before I sing *Hoo-ray and up it rises*, whether ear-lie in the morning or otherwise.

Paul Simmons
Twickenham, Middlesex

SIR - We all know that ships are female, because when they enter the harbour, they head straight for the buoys.

Amanda Rowlands
Lydbrook, Gloucestershire

SIR - My car is a he. His name is Brian because part of his registration is ENO. My previous car was a she. Her name was Elsie because part of her registration was LCU. I think that can be counted as gender equality.

Maureen Shaw
Crowborough, East Sussex

Ducking the difficulty

SIR - Given the risk of "misgendering" a caller in need of assistance, perhaps 999 call handlers should greet callers with "aye-up me duck", and then refer to them in conversation as "me duck".

These friendly terms of address are commonly used in this area for folk of all genders and none.

Terry Lloyd
Derby

SIR - As a new WHSmith manager some years ago, I said to a customer: "Thank you, Madam." She replied: "Don't call me Madam; I haven't got a red light outside my door."

Peter Burt
Ramsgate, Kent

SIR - What is the plural of the supposedly "inclusive" non-word "womxn"? Perhaps it's "female persons". Or the the Scrabble-friendly "womxxn".

Laurie Bradshaw
Bolton, Lancashire

SIR - May I, with all due respect, say that the word "womxn" is utter crxp.

Andrew H.N. Gray
Edinburgh

Tissue of issues

SIR - I see that the PC movement has surfaced again, this time to persuade Kleenex to change the name of their Mansize tissues to Extra Large.

However, casual observation of current trends leads me to believe that "Woman-size" might now more accurately describe the larger version.

Michael Attrill
Battle, East Sussex

SIR - If my mother were alive today she would be relieved to hear that Kleenex boxes can no longer be called "Mansize".

It would avoid the confusion that followed the request she made to her local chemist for a "Mansize box of Tampax".

Judith Hopper
Woking, Surrey

SIR - My husband would rather be known as Man than Extra Large.

T. Lewis (Mrs)
Truro, Cornwall

Survival of the tastiest

SIR - Now that we are rapidly approaching the fireworks season, it was interesting to note an article advertising bonfire bites: "Outdoor bred British pork sausages". What would Charles Darwin's thoughts have been on this phenomenon?

Malcolm Goldie
Hildenborough, Kent

SIR - Until recently I was not aware of how dangerous the profession of cheesemaking appears to be.
The wording on the packaging of my cheese and onion sandwich says: "The farmhouse cheddar cheese in our sandwiches is made from British milk matured for over eight months by generations of cheesemakers".

Tony Cowan
Elgin, Morayshire

Change, in brief

SIR - Many years ago as a helicopter pilot at Staff College, I was made aware of the recent addition of laser-guided bombs (LGBs) to our inventory. Our bomber crews were involved with laser-guided bomb training (LGBT).
Imagine my puzzlement but delight when several

thousand people took to the streets of Manchester last year in noisy support of LGBTQ. It is very encouraging in this era of peace to see that so many should still support the sterling work of our Armed Forces.

Martin Mayer
Chorley, Lancashire

SIR - How much easier it would be to understand the word "miniseries" if it contained a hyphen.

Toni Lewis
King's Lynn, Norfolk

Out of the mouths of babes

SIR - Your story about youth "street speak" is sad, demonstrating the widening gulf between the responsible, communicative adult and the rising generation.
   Honestly, I bonged my peevers over this.

Arthur W.J.G. Ord-Hume
Guildford, Surrey

SIR - Well, so, I am sort of, you know, writing to pass on an idea for getting people to stop saying *well*, and *so*, and *sort of*, and *you know*, in every sentence. A pocket device that reacts every time it hears them? An app for your phone? A deluxe version that reacts whenever a sentence ends on an up note?

Peter Isdell-Carpenter
Alton, Hampshire

SIR - Window shopping near Harvey Nichols, my friend and I passed a Yummy Mummy with a roughly one-year-old child in a pushchair. As she strapped him in she said: "RHETORICAL! Can you say RHETORICAL?"

Veronica Timperley
London W1U

SIR - When I hear Jacob Rees-Mogg saying "Do y' know what?" or "When I was sat", I'll know that all is finally lost.

Gareth Lewis
Blockley, Gloucestershire

DEAR
DAILY TELEGRAPH

The more fool us

SIR - I usually manage to spot your April Fools' Day spoof news item fairly speedily, but I predict that this year's edition will provide me with several highly likely alternatives. This year will also prove particularly difficult for your own editorial staff as they must concoct a sufficiently bizarre story for it to be recognised as such, and not thought of as just another foolhardy action by Westminster's resident court jesters. They, sadly, have made Britain the laughing stock of Europe. I wish you luck.

Hillary Bagshaw
Portsmouth, Hampshire

SIR - As we savour once again the headline "Freddie Starr Ate My Hamster" following the pop star's passing, it may be an appropriate moment to rescue another sub-editorial masterpiece from oblivion: the *News of the World*'s "NUDIST WELFARE MAN'S MODEL WIFE FELL FOR THE CHINESE HYPNOTIST FROM THE CO-OP BACON FACTORY".

Unlike the Freddie Starr story, that was not fake news.

Nicholas Guitard
Bude, Cornwall

As years go by

SIR - I regularly check Today's Birthdays in the *Telegraph* to see who my contemporaries are among the great and the good. However, this does remind me that age is creeping up on me; so you can imagine my despair to find in today's edition that I would have been second in the list had I been distinguished enough to be eligible. Sometimes it is best not to know.

James Harris
Winchester, Hampshire

SIR - Please can you transfer the daily news about Jeremy Corbyn from the front page to the Announcements/Retired page, opposite Obituaries.

Nina Barker
Bordon, Hampshire

SIR - Having recently celebrated my 90th birthday, I have decided not to be upset at not appearing on the Letters page - just so long as I don't appear on the Obituaries page. Perhaps the Editor and I can do a deal.

John Sutton
Newcastle, Staffordshire

Away from the desk

SIR - I have felt disappointed that Alex has been on holiday for such a long time. But then he is a banker, after all.

Robin Nonhebel
Swanage, Dorset

SIR - I'm not sure I can cope with current news stories without Matt to help me interpret them in a sober and realistic way.

Are you sure he is away? Have you looked in all the cupboards? Is his absence fake news?

We'd like him back as soon as possible, please.

Liz Wicken
Cambridge

The camera sometimes lies

SIR - Never mind the Brexit machinations. The thing that puzzles me is the state of Michael Deacon's facial hair. On one column he appears bearded, and on another he is clean-shaven.

Barbara Biggs
London N22

SIR - The steam locomotives recently pictured on your pages are not only a welcome change from actresses or other media personalities. Given that a steam engine never needs Photoshopping to remove facial flaws or body fat, they are also a lot more real.

Graham Breeze
Ilkley, West Yorkshire

SIR - Please could the editors of the sport section take care where they place the photographs, taking into account just where the staples will be.

You recently gave Mary Earps a large nose ring and a lip piercing. Not attractive at all.

Robert Ward
Loughborough, Leicestershire

A little local trouble

SIR – On the weather page, under British readings, you have stopped listing Bradford. Have they stopped having weather?

Maggie Hodd
London W6

SIR – In today's weather section, one sentence starts: "A cold front be across southern Scotland today…"

Can anyone read this without adopting a *Treasure Island* "Arrr Jim" accent?

Rupert Baker
Grateley, Hampshire

SIR – I have decided, after many unsuccessful attempts to get one of my very interesting and topical letters published, to move to Hampshire, as letters from this county feature at least once a day.

Only three today but I am sure there will be more later this week. Hertfordshire certainly does not have as much luck in this regard.

Rosemary Almond
Hoddesdon, Hertfordshire

Yours, puzzled

SIR – Am I getting Alzheimer's or is the Puzzle Page getting more difficult?

Today I am struggling with Codewords and the Tough Sudoku. The news is unread.

Linda Major
London SW15

SIR – The answer to 12 across in yesterday's quick crossword – "Fruit; Nonsense" – was *rhubarb*.

I always thought rhubarb was a vegetable. At least I hope so as I entered my sticks of rhubarb in the vegetable section of our local show.

Lesley Ball
Liskeard, Cornwall

SIR – I experienced a frisson of apprehension on reading the clue in Saturday's Quick Crossword, "Item for sewer". Thank goodness the answer was *needle*.

Sue Thomas
Monmouth

No longer alone in thinking

SIR – I have recently converted to *The Daily Telegraph* following the change of editorship at the *Daily Mail*. As a committed Brexiteer, I have been pleased to find that posh people think along the same lines as me.

Ian Smith
Witham, Essex

SIR – Everyone is entitled to my opinion.

T.P. Davison
Yatton, Somerset

SIR - I consider myself lucky to have never met and married a person like Allison Pearson.

We would never have found anything to disagree about.

Richard Acland
Chepstow, Monmouthshire

SIR - Last night I dreamt that Allison Pearson had become our new prime minister.

Unfortunately, this morning, I awoke to reality.

Bob Millen
Northfleet, Kent

The write stuff

SIR - If only government departments and public bodies were staffed by *Telegraph* letter-writers, this would be a truly delightful country to live in.

Val Strickland
Middlesbrough, North Yorkshire

SIR - My mother used to say you should write your grievances on a piece of toilet paper and flush it down the toilet.

Now she emails her grievances to the Editor - usually at five in the morning, after a frustrated night's sleep.

Katie Hurlow
Weybridge, Surrey

SIR - Rather ambitiously, I made two New Year's resolutions for 2019 - first, to have a letter published in your paper and, second, to visit every Devon pub recommended in the 2019 edition of *The Good Pub Guide*.

I would greatly appreciate your assistance with the former so that I can devote more time to the latter.

Nick Holdsworth
East Ogwell, Devon

SIR - "Disgusted of Tunbridge Wells" seems to have given up recently. Writer's cramp, I suppose.

Alan Duncalf
Bampton, Devon

P.S.

SIR – My attention has been drawn to the effect a recent success I've enjoyed in persuading *The Daily Telegraph* to publish one of my letters has had.

It appears that I may have mistakenly given the impression to friends and family that the Queen, the Prime Minister and the Archbishop of Canterbury are likely to have read, and been influenced by, my work. I now understand this is unlikely to be the case.

As such, please may I ask you to not publish this letter. It will only make me worse.

Mark Allen
East Grinstead, West Sussex

SIR – I have just realised that my chances of literary fame are better if you don't publish my missives. A newspaper is here today and gone tomorrow, but inclusion in one of the volumes of unpublished letters is forever.

Martin Stallion
Braintree, Essex